Building a Handmade Business

Growing a Creative Company

By Patricia Arnold

Written by Patricia Arnold.
Illustrations by Patricia Arnold & Lisa Arnold
Cover design, book formatting and art by Patricia Arnold.
Published by 4 Oak Books.

ISBN: 9781723945694

To the first creative entrepreneur I ever knew. Thanks for the inspiration, Grandma Blanche.

Table of Contents

Creative ENTREPRENUER

creative entrepreneurship - A creative entrepreneurship is the practice of forming a business or becoming self-employed in a creative industry. Creative entrepreneurs are investors in talent.

Creative Entrepreneurs

A creative entrepreneurship is defined as the practice of forming a business or becoming self-employed in a creative industry. Individuals looking into a creative entrepreneurship are likely to discover a career to keep them energized for years. It's a lifestyle I've lived for seventeen years and despite the hard work, it's an experience I recommend. It's an endeavor that will give you confidence, enjoyment and possibly change your life for the better.

A love of art leads imaginative people to investigate a career in creativity. The creative individual who begins a small business envisions a lifestyle of expression while connecting with others who share their enthusiasm for art.

Everyone has their own set of reasons for starting a small business. The motivations range from spending more time with family to wanting an additional source of income. Other reasons include a desire to help others. This is often a great place to begin, because it comes from the desire to make a difference.

Monetizing your creative ideas makes logical sense. For those of us on a budget, selling creative work is a necessary support for art and writing. Being able to afford to buy art supplies or a good laptop to type out your ideas are examples of what can be gained by starting a creative business.

In a world where workers face increasing stress, a career offering creative freedom seems more desirable than ever. Connecting the clear health and emotional benefits of art to a small business can be an ideal work situation.

Art is useful for minds of all ages. Activities such as drawing engage all the senses and wire the brain for successful learning. Cognitive research conducted on a small population of recent retirees between the ages of 62 and 70 concluded that creating art can delay the age-related decline of certain brain functions.

Awareness of the potential consumer market also fuels creative startups. Consumers want to buy handmade goods that have a history and stories to tell. They're drawn to product stories and personal anecdotes. If an artisan has learned how to sew dolls based on their grandmother's pattern, this background story further adds to the appeal of the product. This making old things new again approach to buying provides a wonderful opportunity for artists to find new markets to promote and sell their work.

Creative people are more inspired than ever to build their own company. With the recent influx of customers seeking handmade goods, the timing is right for the creative business. Shifts in consumer demographics seem to agree.

The United States Census Bureau predicts that within a few years, half the population will be age 49 or older. As they age, buyers with connected, mainstream lifestyles haven't forgotten the memories of their youth. This nostalgic urge to bring elements from the past into the present has provided creative entrepreneurs with a growing market for their work.

I like that I can work on my business projects in my spare time. Even if it's for a brief time each day, it feels good to be in charge of recognizing potential and rewarding it. Learning about an art event I can be a part of is an amazing feeling. It keeps me focused and improves my mood when I'm working through other obligations.

Receiving a notification that I've sold a painting serves as confirmation that: A. Years of efforts are being rewarded, B. My art is being seen and shared, and C. This could be an income to offset retirement expenses! I'm thankful every day that I took the time to believe in myself. My improved outlook didn't happen overnight. In fact, it took awhile; but the rewards are well worth the journey.

Of course, technology has played a role in the successes I've had.

The Internet has helped creative people find new markets to sell. For example, artists have access to selling platforms like Etsy if they want to get the word out. Options for online stores abound. From Amazon to Facebook, new marketplaces are arriving on the web every day. Social media drives marketing for creative goods both tangible and digital by providing artists with access to supporters worldwide.

My Creative Story

I've chosen to discuss creative businesses with a focus on art because I've enjoyed creating art since I was young. I've always wanted to be an artist, and my first pictures were drawn inside books my grandmother kept on the shelf. My mother told me I began drawing people at the age of two. This seems incredible, but I do remember scribbling in my grandmother's books. I must have seemed pretty remarkable for them to not caution me against decorating books with my art. My grandmother let me have the book to take home with me.

I've found ways to combine my creative skills to earn additional income. Writing children's stories and drawing my own illustrations are examples of the types of creative pairings I've used.

Since 1999, my goal has been to earn income from my creative endeavors. Over the years, some of my original business dreams yielded to fresh new ideas. Yet, in the past decade, I've founded two companies that are still around today. Ideas are formed and reshaped, but they never end entirely. They become a foundation for what's next, the better version we need.

I've always been an entrepreneur at heart. I always wanted to (at the risk of using a popular catch phrase) be my own boss. I come from a family with the same vision. Many of my relatives have businesses of their own.

The ingenuity shown by those with less is amazing to me.

I'll never forget my grandmother's flea market, Arnold Variety. Well into her fifties, this full time grandmother and part-time clown (a real clown with the handle of Beeper) decided that she wanted to open up a used furniture store in our home town of Owosso, Michigan.

Her business began in the back yard shed she held her garage sales at. Inspired by the sales of her craft items and refurbished furniture,

she rented to a simple building in town and then upgraded to a small warehouse next to a barber shop. She added her amazing creativity to this store.

Grandma Blanche had been sewing doll clothes and making stuffed animals for her children since the 1940's. Although money was tight, I like to think she loved making things because she sewed her whole life. She made her children's clothing and dresses for me to wear.

She encouraged all of us to participate in her business. I still remember the women in the family seated at the table in the store creating giant latch hook rugs for my grandmother to sell. Even my dad, a Vietnam Veteran with his own challenges and responsibilities at his job, got involved in the handmade effort. He carved jewelry boxes by hand from pine, complete with drawers and detailed handles. I would love to have saved just one.

At the age of ten or eleven, I was making illustrations for her to sell. My grandmother hung them proudly on the store walls. I helped to create a sign for the store, but her carefully stenciled white letters on a wooden sheet of plywood painted blue were all her own.

Eventually, my grandmother became ill and couldn't manage her store anymore. The town had moved on to franchises and big box stores. Decades have passed, but I can see our family business in my memories. Though humble compared to the chain stores that have replaced her modest little store, Arnold Variety still makes me proud.

At seventeen, I was fortunate enough to impress my employers at a local grocery store in my home town with my artistic abilities. They allowed me to paint their large front windows during sales and holidays. Eventually, they let me create price signs every Friday. I look upon those days as golden opportunities to avoid stocking shelves and bagging groceries.

After graduating from high school, I decided to offer my art services to the public. I made fliers announcing my skills as a pet portrait artist. I had one customer lead the entire year. After a presentation at a car dealership that could have went better, I learned something about being prepared. After refining my approach and with some help with art supplies from my mother, I began to go to craft shows and sell my work.

It was slow going at first, but eventually customers began buying my hand painted apparel and requesting custom orders. When I had difficulty finding ways to promote my work, I learned how important accessibility in the marketplace was. This problem became painfully clear when I had trouble finding a gallery willing to show my art even after selling a large color pencil work at the same venue.

I find rejection to be comparable to an annoying person who wants to keep you in your place even when you're not willing to stay there. Even though the rejections I've received over the years seem unwarranted and even mean spirited, each "no" adds to my determination. To past disappointments, I say this: my plans haven't changed.

After some soul searching, I decided my goal is to get my art into the hands of the people.

As a young woman of very limited means, I felt limited by my lack of connections and limited by my surroundings. Certain I wouldn't make any headway selling art alone, I found a related field and then forgot about my dream. However, I believe that because I was given this gift, the path I embarked on away from art eventually lead me right back to it. Art is instinct, and it's always there. Even though I took the long way, I arrived at the same destination.

In high school I often walked up town after school and used the money I made babysitting to buy individual Berol Prismacolor coloring pencils. Each one cost about eighty-nine cents, and I was wearing them down quite fast. In the late 1980's, my mother took me to the shopping mall to buy art supplies at a time when they were steeply priced indeed. She invested in my talent by buying me that extra nice set of color pencils and a matte cutter, a kindness I'll never forget.

I wouldn't apply the term starving artist to myself, but when my first daughter was born, money was in short supply. By 2000, I found myself a single parent of two children with little resources. Even with a college education, I couldn't find a sustainable job in graphic design.

When I did find employment, in no way did I feel creative making minimum wage with zero creative control. Working as a graphic designer, I discovered that much of my job was pulling up stock images and pasting them into documents.

I think Andy Warhol would have been very disappointed if he wasn't allowed to alter the ordinary into something extraordinary. After attempts to inject my own art into ads was roundly rejected, I realized something about myself.

I am an art rebel.

Tired of feeling burdened financially and suffering from blandness in the workplace, I decided to do something about it. Without resources to build my company, I was tasked with the job of literally build something out of nothing. I immediately focused on the positive. I already had two assets, creativity and the desire to better my situation for my family.

My children were a great motivator, so with a non-existent budget, I started with what I knew. My two year degree in design wouldn't be quite enough. Experience was needed. Looking to build my portfolio, I accepted graphic design projects for minimum wage.

Just before the Great Recession, I had achieved some success in my field and I was gaining clients. As the number of projects began to pile up, I began to consider hiring employees or training family members to work for me. However, it wasn't long before everything seemed to stall after the arrival of crowd sourced design marketplaces.

Thousands entered the arena of graphic design. Whether they were graphic designers or they were self-taught, they offered businesses lower priced options. They were willing to do design not just cheaply, but free. Some offered logos comprised of templates they simply changed the text on. It wasn't that I looked down on the designers that chose this route, but I couldn't compete with crowd sourced design and I didn't want to.

When faced with situations like this, I recall a movie quote from Kate the Armorer from A Knight's Tale. At some point, William is trying to get his armor fixed and she tells him she doesn't work for free. In frustration he tells her he can't joust without the repair, to which she replies, "Your problem, not mine. Each droplet of sweat has a price on it."

I'm not implying that art and making armor is equally stressing to the body, but I feel we should all value what we produce if we've spent hours perfecting it.

After a major disappointment with a particularly demanding client, I decided to rethink the field I had chosen. Updating my skills made sense at the time. I went back to college to learn web development. Other than learning to code, designing websites wasn't much different than graphic design. However, I learned it had similar pitfalls.

With projects that grew in scope beyond what was manageable, I began to question how long I could hold out. Every time I thought something was done, I had to learn a new programming language.

To make matters more challenging, technology was moving faster than I was. Plenty of designers couldn't find work at all and once again, I was no exception. I kept trying to update my skills, but it didn't matter which programming language I learned, employers were perpetually looking for something else. Forever facing a skills mismatch, I wondered if anyone cared about creativity any more. It was time to hit the pause button. Burning out my brain cells to keep up with the latest development tech fad wasn't working for me.

Eventually, I found myself approaching forty and nearing the completion of a master's degree in computer science. Even with a major achievement on the horizon, I still felt doubtful. I was still uncertain about the future. I pondered the same questions. When would I finally decide I had learned enough to get started on an actual career? Or more to the point, when would my abilities be good enough for the elusive dream job I was looking for?

Sometimes an unusual event can be the catalyst. In my case, it was a meeting with a costumed psychic at a popular amusement park. After drawing a card in the spirit of fun, she told me that there was something I had always wanted to do since I was a child. She advised that I shouldn't worry, that I should take a chance. It was a vague fortune to be sure, but one that made me think.

I had once wanted to be a writer and illustrator of my own books.

It wasn't long after that that I founded a small independent publishing company. After finding success selling books often co-written by my family, I decided to go back to my roots.

Writing and designing ebooks utilized my college education, but something was still missing. My years moving a mouse and typing on a keyboard had evolved into repetitive stress injuries such as carpal tunnel and even a condition of the forearms known as Cubital Tunnel Syndrome.

It seemed I was in need of a higher range of movement, so in 2015, I began a home-based handmade arts and crafts business, dividing my time between both ventures. Initially in it for my health, I was delighted when my creations began to sell.

My body and my mind were both thanking me with a reward of less pain. Sculpting clay figurines helped the flexibility in my hands. Mentally, unplugging brought peace of mind. My eating habits improved and so did my back pain. In essence, I was embracing my original dream of being an artist creating works on canvas, paper and wood.

This wasn't to say I had abandoned technology completely. I've never been happier doing graphic and web design because I finally found the elusive design client with projects that engage my creativity. Of course, the client I'm talking about is me. The time I spent learning hasn't been wasted, I just needed to change my approach. I've been drawing, painting, woodburning, sculpting, block printing and screen printing my way through life ever since.

A Creative Way of Life

"You're mad, bonkers ... but I'll tell you a secret: All the best people are."

- Alice in Wonderland

While not necessarily referring to myself as bonkers, my creative path has been an unusual one. While on this journey, I've learned a lot about selling handmade. When I look back, there's a great deal of information I wish I had known about when I first began as a creative entrepreneur. With this book, I hope to at least shorten the learning curve.

I also hope to answer some of the questions I get from family members, friends, and people I meet without missing important details. After having a conversation with someone about my work, I often discover that I forgot to tell them something helpful. This book is my opportunity to provide advice and background about creative companies.

When I talk about my creative businesses to others, I enter the conversation concerned about how unusual it must seem to others that I've chosen this lifestyle. When people are interested enough to ask questions, it dawns on me that I'm not the only one inspired. Just about everyone I speak to knows of someone in need of information about selling their art.

I'm hoping this book will give you a new perspective or at least confirm what you've always known. Choosing a creative way of life will leave you feeling energized. Because there's so much enjoyment in it, the day has more possibilities than usual.

In the beginning, you may feel apprehensive about sharing your work. This is completely normal, but most people have already guessed that you have talent so there's no use in hiding it. You're probably the artistic one your friends and family tell others about. The compliments you receive about something you've created serve as confirmation that you have a captive audience.

Some of the artists I meet are interested in selling their handmade items for the first time. I've also spoken to people in the technical or medical field who just want to have an outlet for their creativity. These professionals may be nearing retirement or they just want to participate in something that feels less stressful.

In this book, I'll provide an overview of the resources I've used for positive results. I want to be clear that none of these techniques have made me a millionaire (as of now), but I'm better off than I was before and I want this to be your experience as well. I want you to be successful at being inspired.

In summation, I'm hoping I'll persuade you to have faith in your creativity.

Perhaps you're uncertain if there's a market for your work. I like to think there are artists who agree with me on the topic of independent inspiration. For example, I enjoy drawing subjects that intrigue me. The good news for those of us who chart their own course is that there are buyers interested in something unique.

Creative Mentors

Of course, there are doubters that will disagree. They're usually the ones that are skeptical of your ability to make a living. An apparent lack of enthusiasm from those around you will sow seeds of doubt in your mind. It can be frustrating because it's not that you don't understand that what you're trying to attempt is difficult. Facing the objections can be an uphill battle, especially when people are worried and don't understand how you'll get by financially.

Creative mentors can keep your inspiration and confidence soaring.

When I graduated with a high school diploma in 1988, starting a career in art was a difficult endeavor. Just getting accepted at an art college was a lot of work. I had to put my art work on slides for the admissions department to review. It was such a lengthy process that I had to overnight a packed envelope just to get my application to a university on time.

As an aside, my high school art teacher helped me prepare my materials and even paid for shipping. She was always there with an encouraging word. These are the types of mentors every creative person needs around them, and I'll always be grateful to my art teachers and professors. Each has influenced me to have faith in myself and my work.

I recently found my picture in a Freshman yearbook in a town I lived in prior to moving to another town. When I see my young smiling face, I think the creative ideas I had and my hopes for the future. I also remember my Freshman art teacher and how she told me my art had potential. I found her in the yearbook as well, and she looked exactly as I remembered her because I recall the faces of those who encouraged me.

I also remember my middle school art teacher well. She introduced me to different types of media I hadn't considered before and showed me how to shade and highlight. With her guidance, I was designing the cover of the school yearbook and planning the school mural.

My memory is so vivid when it comes to positive mentoring I've been fortunate to receive, that I could go all the way back to early childhood education (but I won't!). The point is, I remember the faces of my creative mentors because the inspiration they gave me has made an impact on my life. The world will continue to be a better place because of their presence in it.

Before getting upset over a lack of support and letting worries get the best of you, think about who you are as a creative person. Most people are aware of the financial challenges but have decided to start the journey regardless of any obstacles. Even if I have just a day to spare to work on it or even a few hours, I've found that being artistic is in my soul. I have to go where inspiration leads whenever I can.

From my own personal experience, being creative is something that made me a whole person. Being an artist was something that kept me going. A friend in difficult times, my art is the best thing I have to share.

Besides, I'm not sure anyone remembers how well I packed groceries in a bag or stocked products on a shelf, but they do remember my art work. People recall art because it's memorable. It's one of the first things people talk about when we meet. Every now and then, I learn that they still have the drawings I made as far back as high school.

To me, that means something.

Monetizing Art

Even if we're feeling amazing giving the world the results of our creative inspirations, we still need to pay the bills right? Of course! So let's discuss what you can achieve with your talents.

When trying to monetize your creative abilities, it's good to think about the position of art in the world today. Creativity is everywhere! It's not the stereotype vocation of haughty, shallow types. A graphic designer created the graphics you see on television and an artist painted the stunning mural in the hotel lobby. Someone creative planned the design of your furniture and your house.

I can guarantee you that an artist, graphic designer and writer created the book you're reading now (without a team). If there's a need for something creative, there's an opportunity. If your creative item helps people aesthetically or provides a function such as learning or offers utility, there will be someone who wants to buy it.

Whether you write books filled with knowledge and entertainment or make handmade products, as a creative entrepreneur you have an opportunity to fill this need. With the proper attention, the sales of your creative products will gain in momentum.

Before getting started, ask yourself three basic questions. What kind of creative product will you make? How can you make it a good fit for potential customers? Furthermore, how will you spread the word about it?

If you're an artist, you could publicize your paintings for sale. If you create a unique handmade item, you'll want to reach the right group of potential customers. Regardless of your route to success, it's good to produce a plan. I've included some exercises in this book to work on in the coming pages.

Hire Yourself

People founding creative businesses come from many different backgrounds. Some are beginning their careers as fine artists, designers or somewhere in between. Some have tried to sell their work in the past. Maybe they didn't have the success they expected and wish to try again. Maybe they're looking for a reset or advice on where to best focus their energies. Like me, maybe you want to start a creative business as an outlet to improve your health and outlook.

Creative entrepreneurs are building a road map to success depending on their perspective.

Regardless of your point of view, you'll be relieved to know that selling your creative works to the public doesn't have to cost a large amount of money or require a bank loan. For those who find themselves in difficult financial times, this is a refreshing bit of news. The desire to sell your work comes from a need to sustain your creativity in a way that allows you to continue what you love the most: creating.

Getting heavily into debt doesn't allow for this. However, a measure of creative talent, flexible thinking and confidence make all the difference. This underscores an important point. Creative people must make sensible business decisions. I've used techniques in the past requiring little or no investment other than time. I've had many challenges, but I've also had an equal amount of success.

It's a great idea to utilize what you already have to build a small business that can sustain itself. If you've given some thought to your creative business, you've probably already determined you'll have to work hard to achieve your goals. I'm not going to dissuade you from this conclusion, because both hard work and dedication are required.

Even if you haven't thousands or even hundreds of dollars to begin your creative business, a lack of funds needn't sideline your dream. However, making expensive mistakes will impede your efforts. Before you decide to try borrowing against your future, wouldn't it be a good idea to take stock of what you already bring to the table?

If your experiences are anything like mine, you lack a pile of cash to get started. However, with a creative eye, a knowledge of what people like and capable hands you have the makings of something great. Pair these abilities with knowing your way around the Internet and you have more than enough to get started monetizing your creations!

My Creative Roles

1. Founder
2. Graphic Designer
3. Artist
4. Creative Director
5. Author
6. Marketer
7. Miscellaneous (as needed)

My Skills

1. Artistic skills
2. Writing skills
3. Experienced in Computers
4. Marketing background
5. Graphic design background

Utilizing skills you already have will help your fledgling company stay within a strict budget. Having a degree is helpful, but real world experience is also of benefit. Consider the types of skills you're best at.

While considering your skills, make some connections between the ones that you're good at. For instance, I'm a graphic designer, painter, illustrator and writer. Each connection is one more way you can utilize your abilities to build your business.

Perhaps you're fortunate enough to be artistic and outgoing. If you've ever worked with the public, you'll find it easier to be in a selling situation. If you're a natural communicator, then you already realize that customers want to support the business of someone they like.

Note: I would never dissuade my fellow introverts! There are many roles that are ideal for creatives who prefer solitude as they work. Besides, we can always delegate some of the more social tasks to our friends, the extroverts.

Enjoy creating graphics? Technical skills in graphic design or desktop publishing can provide for low cost advertising materials for your business. If you know your way around social media, you may be able to handle marketing tasks yourself.

Below is an exercise that will allow you to list and categorize your skills in a way that is helpful to your creative business.

Exercise 1: Skills

Create a list in a similar format as the example in the image below. If your business has partners or if it's a family business like mine, have each member fill out a worksheet. The first row is an example entry.

Begin by making a list of your abilities. Write as many abilities as you can, filling each box in the first column. Each skill needn't be a professional one. You can be as specific or as general as you like. Don't forget to add skills such as sales. Other suggestions for this column include: Ebay seller, IT, artist, parent, etc.

When you're finished with the abilities column, work on the tasks column. Match each one of your abilities to a business task and write it in the box. Some suggestions include: I can tell people about my work, I can keep track of sales, I can make things to sell, I know what other parents are looking for, I'm able to list products online, etc.

After finishing the tasks column, work on the third column. Create a job title for each task you've written in the purposes column and write it in the box next door. Examples include: Creative director, social media marketer, graphic designer, illustrator, author and editor.

Next, review the list you've built and consider the connections.

Each skill you've added translates into something helpful to a creative business. This equals money saved in expenses.

Learning to adapt to a changing budget is an important skill for an entrepreneur to master. Although you're investing your own time, hiring outside talent requires resources you may not have initially. In addition, this money saving strategy allows you to begin immediately. Building the foundations of your business also adds a personal imprint. By hiring yourself first, you can create a company culture for others to follow in the future.

Building a company is a learning experience. Working in each position allows you to familiarize yourself with your company's structure from top to bottom. You'll learn to alter your approach as needed and improve the quality of the products you sell. You'll discover firsthand which strategies work and which ideas could use improvement. In addition, you're laying the groundwork for how your company will run in the future.

There are a couple caveats for the do-it-yourselfer to consider. Hiring yourself doesn't diminish the possibility of hiring someone else for a task in the future when the continued success of your business demands it. It also goes without saying that hiring a professional for certain tasks is necessary. The purpose of this exercise is to promote confidence in your skill set and to take stock of what you can do personally to contribute to your business.

Priorities

The most important tasks such as making, selling and promoting products are main priorities. This exercise addresses three of the most important components of a creative business: production, distribution and marketing. There are numerous responsibilities when it comes to maintaining a small business, but in the initial planning stages it's helpful to simplify things a bit.

Product ideas build inventory. Based on ideas and made by hand, inventory is what will keep your business afloat. If the production time for one handmade item is too long, a product line can be created based on a single creation. For instance, I can think of at least three products to sell based on one painting. I can scan the original work of art at a high resolution and offer prints for sale such as greeting cards. Considering the time required for each painting, discovering ways to create inventory from a single work of art allows for repeated sales.

Distribution is defined as the action or process of supplying goods to stores and other businesses that sell to consumers. Distribution can be considered as the where and how products will be sold. There are many distribution channels for handmade items such as stores, online platforms and local events. Places for selling creative products might include online marketplaces like Etsy, a nearby farmer's market or a shelf at a local gift shop. Of course, many other options exist.

Marketing is defined as the action or business of promoting and selling products or services, including market research and advertising. They include but aren't limited to print advertising, word of mouth, social media sharing and product giveaways.

Opportunities to promote are always available. Some marketing can be done for free. For example, I share my items for sale on at least four different social media platforms using applications on my mobile phone. This saves time and makes marketing tasks easier. Keeping these three subjects in mind, it's great to organize ideas. Exercise 2 should help you along.

Exercise 2: Organizing

Organize tasks in order of importance. In column one, begin with a product you've made or an idea for a product. In column two, list different ways to sell the same item (if possible). For instance, if you create art, you might list prints, greeting cards, t-shirts, etc. This may include services that promote your work such as teaching a class on the subject.

Column three is for considering different approaches for promoting your product. Ideas include social media sharing, blog posts, attending author events and selling at craft shows.

This exercise was intended as a way to help organize ideas. Don't be surprised if you come up with ideas faster than you can write them down. For creative entrepreneurs, inspiration is the whole point!

Finding Supporters and Patrons

Find a need and fill it. - Ruth Stafford Peale

I was introduced to the above quote by the professor teaching my first business class. I probably forgot most of the details from that long ago Introduction to Business course, but that phrase has remained on my mind. Like trying to solve a riddle, I've tried to figure out how it applies to art. I couldn't figure out how my talents could fill any need other than something to look at.

It was only after I began to listen to what people were telling me that I understood. Your customers and supporters are closer than you think. Not only do they enjoy looking at your work but they have an idea of how they'll use it in their space.

Recently, I sold a piece of art featuring farming equipment. The buyer's intent was to gift it to a family member who owned a business so that he could hang it in his shop. My art now serves as a conversation piece for customers entering his store. This was a purpose for my work I had never considered before.

When it comes to finding patrons, think about anyone who has ever complimented your work or encouraged you. These individuals will mostly likely be your first customers. Your supporters may be family or friends or someone you met at a craft show who admired your work. Events and everyday encounters are a great opportunity to share your business card, social media profile or website. You'll also find encouragement from other artists and makers who can provide a wealth of information on artist friendly places.

Because art can encompass or create a mood, art forges a connection. Making social connections with others is a motive for sharing art, because talking about creative works leads to thought-provoking conversation. These discussions are important because they encourage others to be creative and invest in the arts.

Artists can find encouragement in groups, through word of mouth and networking with like minded individuals. The most beneficial advice I've received is from fellow artists and makers. I follow as many artists as possible on social media because I've been able to learn from their thoughts, approaches to selling and experiences.

Groups on Facebook has been beneficial because I am able to join others who share my interest in pyrography for example. In addition, I have found useful information from groups of artists who sell on the same platforms that I do. Reading this shared knowledge is a great way to learn about opportunities and information you wouldn't have known about otherwise.

Customers come in all forms. It may seem surprising to consider that you already have built in customers! Perhaps it's a friend who has always supported your work or a teacher you drew a picture for years ago. Remember your neighbor from years ago who bought one of your paintings? These are the examples of the people you know who can help you build a customer base.

First of all, make sure to let your friends, family and acquaintances know that you're selling your work. It may seem difficult to "toot your own horn" at first, but if people don't know your work is available to the public, then how can they give you support?

Just when I thought there wasn't much of a market for my art, I found a fan base in my friends. I was asked to create a drawing for a tattoo. I completed the illustration, and my friend was very happy with the design and asked for more. Not only did she order more, but this led to more orders from her friends. Not to mention the tattoos are a conversation piece whenever they're revealed. Never underestimate how far your creativity will reach beyond the influence of friends. It truly can start with one friend sharing your art with others they know and meet. I learned how important it is to value your supporters. Especially if they're close to home. I probably never would have started at all if it wasn't for my mother believing in my talent.

Handling Rejection

Early on, I learned that people have different perspectives. Someone viewing your modern art piece may prefer realism. Not everyone will understand or appreciate your creative vision, but there people that will! Like the individual, art can be personal, so artists understandably take rejection personal as well.

Because it's impossible to please everyone, it's best to focus on groups you can best persuade to view, purchase and share your work positively. Early in my career as an artist, I was trying to get my work out to everyone I could without researching the venue. I spent hours and money driving my paintings from gallery to gallery as if my art was a one-size-fits-all solution.

It was only when I looked deeper into the rejections did I understand my errors.

My first rejection occurred because I hadn't paid attention to the fact I was trying to show my work at a modern art exhibition when my work was more about realism. This was a rookie mistake and an example of a need to research the art event. These misunderstandings can be avoided by learning more about the venue, the types of art shown there and the purpose of the event.

Another situation caused hurt feelings. I had sold one illustration at a local gallery so I felt encouraged to sell more at the same place. After dropping off my art for a juried art show, I received a letter that my work had been rejected and it was time to pick it up. I have to admit, the rejection made me feel annoyed.

In another episode, a gallery representative once asked me if I had copied my work from a photograph. It was too ridiculous to consider. The individual in question actually suggested my whitetail deer was exactly like one she had seen in a photograph. If you're from Michigan, you probably know that white tailed deer look very similar to each other.

I even went through a stage I refer to as matting and framing limbo. I was told my work needed matting and framing. I assumed this was the reason why they wouldn't show my work. Surely, if I just made this adjustment, I could go back to selling my work, right? No. After spending nearly a hundred dollars in a town frame shop guess what my reward was? Zilch. The colors were wrong, the frame was wrong, and so on. Trying to predict an art buyer's taste in matting and framing was like trying to hit a moving target.

When I sell artwork, I prefer to sell it unframed so the buyer can decide what works for them.

As a result of these obstacles, I gave up showing my work locally (and anywhere really) for years. After all, if nearby galleries weren't interested, who would be? Still young, I told myself I had much more to learn. I told myself that maybe I just wasn't that good enough yet. I decided to return to college. I wasn't long in my painting classes before I was given honest feedback that absolutely shouted, YOU ARE GREAT AT THIS!

I remember driving home after class and feeling like I was a cloud. I had received so much encouragement from the instructors and my fellow art students. It seemed I was good enough after all. Needless to say, I could have learned this without paying tuition if I would have just had faith in myself and my art.

As I look back at these experiences, I know my decision to give up displaying my work was a wrong one and the reason for my trouble is that I had forgotten all about niche marketing. It's best to promote your products to the groups of people that would be the most interested. Broadly shipping it to everyone risks art work not being valued.

I regret every penny I spent trying to satisfy an audience that had already said no to my work over and over. Many denials will never equal an acceptance in the minds of those who have decided your work isn't a good fit for their event.

And guess what? That's okay!

There's no reason for hard feelings. When I faced with a rejection recently, I just laughed it off. I know now that this particular business simply wasn't the right place for me to sell my work. It's probable that the owner knows what kind of work sells best at their gallery. My work and this gallery are simply a mismatch.

When seeking a place to sell your art, precision is required. Rejection can save time and money. It's preferable to find a location that is emphatic about your art rather than cope with a lack of enthusiasm.

I have come to believe that the business you enlist to show your work wants you to consider what it is about their gallery or event that appeals to you before you apply. Rushing around takes a lot of energy and it causes those who would really enjoy your work to miss it entirely!

In short, it's easy to miss the forest for the trees.

It's helpful to discuss an event with artists who have had positive or negative experiences. Use a search engine, read reviews and find artist discussions on the location. You may find a wonderful opportunity or save yourself a lot of heartache. Consider your work as worth every bit of the price you're asking for it. Take it seriously, have confidence in it and have a certainty that there is a home for your art for sale, but it might take some time to find it.

Categorizing art and handmade items correctly can reduce rejection. Naturally, I won't be sending realistic paintings of people to a modern art show nor will I try to show my work in a gallery I perceive may miss the entire point of my work or may have a bias. These days, I tend to do some research on the company, event or business entity before applying.

I like to visit a gallery or attend an event first to decide if it would be a place my work will thrive at. First I'm a customer, then I'm a seller. Using this approach, I'm able to take measure of the venue I would like to sell at. Acquaintances and friends that like your work can also provide introductions. They may know of a business that is looking for handmade items to show in their store. In this case, it's good to ask for recommendations from your growing pool of patrons and supporters.

It's inevitable that your art will be turned down, but it's okay. Each rejection provides you with an unexpected opportunity. It's an experience you can add to your list of lessons learned, so that when a YES arrives you can leave those rejections in the rear view mirror.

Reviews

On the topic of reviews, if you sell online, there are bound to be misunderstandings on behalf of buyers. It's frustrating as a seller, but it needn't be the thing that closes your business. You may find a one star review from a customer on your Etsy storefront, for example.

After comparing the tactics of ignoring the comment versus responding, I realized there was very little if anything I could do that would keep things positive and professional. Sometimes the criticisms were helpful (such as pointing out a production flaw). I used the constructive criticism to reflect. Recently, I received a review of an item that helped me improve my manufacturing method.

Other reviews were negative comments with nothing substantive to say. I didn't feel like enforcing this negativity by apologizing for a criticism that didn't have any merit. In the new age of trolling, the best thing I've found to do is to keep the criticism you find beneficial and it's important to realize that some mean to disrupt. In the past I've had to limit access to a web page because of hacking attempts. I consider my online website a storefront just like brick and mortar establishment would be.

It goes without saying that a seller should handle any customer issues carefully and professionally. It helps to learn how others have handled situations you are facing. I've been able to discover good advice on how to handle returns, create a store policy and otherwise find information I've needed from seller discussions on social media. I've been able to reach out to customer support on the platform I'm selling on for advice and assistance. In short, take some time to consider the options before replying negatively.

Think about your response in terms of the effects responding in kind could produce. Prolonging a negative conversation isn't the best for your confidence. Remind yourself that by and large, people like your work and this individual is most likely an exception.

When you're on the receiving end, you can do one or two things. Either move on or explain yourself carefully. When it comes to online reviews, I usually just make a note of any constructive comments and forget the rest. If the comments are personal attacks, more steps are necessary such as reporting the individual. This is an unfortunate situation, but it does happen.

Trolling has become more and more of an issue, and you certainly have the right to inform customer support. That being said, many platforms have a policy of not removing the negative feedback unless they deem it necessary. On Amazon for example, reviews sometimes stay in place even when they seem unfair. Sometimes, it's best to move on. Your fan base is waiting on your next great work after all! If you've done your best to sooth the customers ruffled feathers to no avail, it may be time to focus on those that truly appreciate your efforts. These individuals are likely to outnumber those in the opposing column.

Product Focus

Sellers with a lot of experience in selling handmade recommend avoiding selling many items with different themes. Initially, I offered a hundred items in my handmade store. I sold jewelry with tumbled stone, hair accessories, paintings, painted t-shirts, screenprinted items along with woodburned items large and small. Next, I added sculpted figurines and hand pulled prints.

As you can imagine, my store was getting cluttered. Some recommended opening additional stores to cover each theme. Judging by my changing interests, I would have had to build and promote ten stores. Since I didn't want to spread myself too thin, I decided to stay with one store.

I was new to the process. Since my crafts business began as a part time project, I was willing to observe
the results for awhile. Within a year, I discovered which items garnered interest and which items were not selling.

Everyone wants to succeed in their business, but they may lack the right information. My experiment provided me with an important marketing analysis. Throwing every idea out there to see what sticks seems sloppy, but I don't regret it.

The information I discovered applied to sales. Learning how customers found my products and which items were the most popular allowed me to hone my approach and finally focus. I now offer products in four categories: prints, paintings, woodburnings and figurines.

I don't recommend this haphazard approach as something everyone should do. In fact, if I could have done things over I would have only offered products in one theme and then waited it out before adding another.

My first year was a road of discovery, and I've made some errors. Having many different types of products was one of them, but it didn't kill my business. I learned something, and I adjusted my approach and focused on as few themes as my creative mind could manage. I wouldn't change that first year for anything. I have a more focused, leaner handmade store than I began with.

Advice I've read indicates that even four types of products is too much. For artists like myself who do more than one type of art, it's a miracle I was able to narrow the focus this much. A good approach is to choose the items that sell the most. Booming sales are a wonderful motivator,

For me, the answer to this dilemma wasn't separation of themes, it was organizing my store. For example, Etsy allows sellers to have "departments" in their store. I place each type of product in the matching section. As a result, my store is organized.

What is the unifying factor between paintings, prints, figurines and woodburned items? In a word, it's me. I have made each one of these items, I've received good feedback on them and each sell in equal amounts. I wouldn't want to maintain four stores and I don't want to add another set of marketing responsibilities. For me, diversifying with focus was effective because I am engaged in interested in these types of products.

Obstacles

– time

One of the biggest obstacles to starting a business is time. For those of us not gifted with a fortune in start-up money, we have responsibilities that can't be ignored. It's not prudent to quit your job when it's the income you rely on to pay the bills. When continuing your day job is necessary, it may help to keep your creative endeavors somewhere in the back of your mind as you work. It's the light that brightens the mundane, the potential reminding you of your unique contribution to the world.

Rather than giving up art or giving up a job, I decided to compromise between the two. Even though I was working on my dream part time, I felt I was making some progress even if it wasn't rapid. As my books and art have become more successful, I've been able to reduce hours.

Here is an example of my current schedule: When I wake up, I'm checking email. After that, I concentrate on which one of my projects are closest to completion and focus on that one. I usually work for a couple hours a day. I work in the late afternoon and evenings so I can devote my mornings to building my small business. When work is over, I'm attending to the needs of my family but sometimes get an opportunity to create art or write some more.

This may seem like quite a division, but it's amazing how much I can get done towards my creative business each day with two hours of dedication. This schedule requires the right frame of mind. For awhile, I suffered from insomnia because of all the ideas I wanted to explore but didn't have time to work on. My current approach is to write these ideas down so I don't forget them. This allows me to revisit the best ones later when I have more time. Getting to bed on time makes my mornings more productive.

As your creative works begin to pay off, you can reduce your work hours by that amount. Often employers don't wish to work with these requests, but my current job is a work at home position that allows me more freedom. I had to switch jobs many times until I found the right arrangement. Each employer is different, however, and it can be hard to find a suitable schedule.

For me, creating art became the luxury I could have vs. money I could spend. Time is sometimes the best indulgence you can give yourself if you're an artist. In other words, I'm willing to forgo an expensive vacation in exchange for time in the studio.

The goal then becomes at what point can I just be creative for a living? Keeping that milestone in your mind will keep you motivated with your eyes on the prize: a lifestyle where you can do what you love full time.

- money

We've been led to believe that businesses can only begin with a big investment. I've heard stories of entrepreneurs taking a mortgage out on their home or even borrowing money from a relative. Loan ads to begin a business abound on the Internet. I receive offers in my mail box with promises of a guaranteed loan. Not wishing to be in debt, I chased grant opportunities on the web only to come up empty handed.

I knew I had a strong idea and the talent to thrive, but I didn't have the money to purchase advertising or to create a strong local marketing campaign. When I thought about these obstacles, it made me depressed. Feeling down about your vision is no way to begin.

By 2000, I was a single mother of two beautiful girls. I had ambition and talent, but I didn't have money. I certainly couldn't break into any local art scene, I didn't have the influence. However, I was willing to build.

Without a staff and without any means to pay for services, I became my own customer. I was having trouble finding work. Fresh from earning an Associate Degree in Graphic Communications, it took me over a year to find a part time job. The pay was meager and I learned the hard way that job security was rare. I worked while pregnant only to find my job given to someone else when I returned from maternity leave.

It made me sad to think that all the hard work studying at college would lead to something I couldn't even depend on.

To be honest, I'm not the most consistent worker. I'm also a little rebellious when I don't agree with the direction of a project. I chalk it up to my temperament, which is a bit more lackadaisical than some. My first grade teacher described me as a "free spirit" with good reason. Naturally, I took this as a compliment. I believe that people are the happiest and the most productive doing what they love.

I used my education as a graphic designer to create advertising and websites. Being my own client allowed me to save on these services. While I wasn't getting paid, I didn't need to borrow money to buy these things from someone else.

If you're willing to invest your time, you can save a tremendous amount. Perhaps your talent lies in writing. You can leverage this skill by writing your own ad copy and website content. Doing these tasks in the beginning allows you to explore your passion for your business.

Framing your new business as a "stock" you're investing in can be reassuring that your time isn't wasted. Those of us who have made even modest investments in the stock market know that over time, if all goes well, your stock will most likely increase in value. In essence, the things you create are your stocks, your investment in yourself.

A little patience and skill today can help you save for tomorrow. Every royalty check I receive or painting I sell is a reminder to me that with every book I write or art work I paint, I am creating financial security for myself. Don't be afraid to set aside some time to invest in your future. You'll be glad you did and you won't even have to pay a brokerage fee.

Even if sales don't instantly materialize, keep working anyways. Those works you produce will sell at some point and the more things you have for sale, the higher your sales will be. Continue to produce your best work for your creative "bank" and you'll have something to offset a rainy day.

– indecision

Sometimes it's difficult to decide that starting a business is the right thing to do. Enter another obstacle, indecision. You may have reservations about your ability to be successful or whether you can spare the time. I had these same worries and decided to take an inventory of the reasons why I should start a business and why I shouldn't. The positives column was much longer than the negatives column and easier to create.

However, spending my spare time on an artistic endeavor to earn money seemed risky. Shouldn't I be working all the time? Wasn't that what I was supposed to do? We certainly needed every dime of my paycheck. How could I be sure it all would be worth my while?

Sometimes there are elements that make a forty hour work week difficult. I had two small children, occasional transportation problems and some health issues. These were some of the factors that led me to the decision to be my own boss. Things haven't been easy, but I've been able to spend more time with my children while maintaining a better work/life balance.

If you've ever purchased stocks, you incur a certain amount of risk. Some of those stocks may be in companies that won't last or under perform. For me, it made more sense to invest in my own abilities. I consider my art and handmade products to be my "stocks". Initially, the buy in is inexpensive as the currency is time. With sales of my art increasing, it seems what began as a part time business has evolved into something more.

Most artists begin creating art as a pastime. Perhaps they went to a painting or pottery class and discovered they were good at it. Whether this is a later in life discovery or an artistic gift, it's likely the creative gene has always existed in one form or another.

Selling artwork can support creativity. Sales can help purchase art supplies such as new brushes, canvas or those expensive paints we would love to try. Regardless of the size of the reward, the incentives are there.

- fear

"Nothing ventured, nothing gained." - Benjamin Franklin

This Benjamin Franklin quote rings true. You can't expect to achieve anything if you never take any risks at all.

I think that fear is the biggest obstacle, and I've experienced two types. The first type of fear is a fear of failure. For years, I didn't want to submit anything out of fear of being judged. After successfully making it through college I learned that not everyone will appreciate my efforts. This reality is built into the fabric of life.

As a creative person, I've been through artist's critiques in art class. An artist critique is an oral or written discussion strategy used to analyze, describe, and interpret works of art. Through every critique, I've had a surplus of positive remarks along with more critical comments.

At first, I dreaded critiques because they seemed a overly harsh. There were times when I would agree with someone's input. There were also times when it seemed a cartoon conversation bubble could appear over my head with a question mark.

Some of the criticism seemed like the person providing a critique couldn't think of what to say about my work so they just said the first comment that popped into their head. This makes sense because no one want to hurt anyone's feelings. I can't determine if I feel there is any value in a critique. Even honest feedback can result in hurt feelings if the artist isn't accustomed to it.

I remember an architectural drawing class I was in. I became anxious when it seemed my work was deeply criticized. At the age of eighteen, it bothered me so much I didn't return to class. Years later in another art class, the same professor told me that he didn't remember me being this good.

When we discussed my previous drawing issues, he told me all I had to do was draw the negative space. I smile when I think about how complicated I had made things. It turned out that I didn't need a class in perspective when all I have to do is paint things as I see them. Imagine if Grandma Moses would have obsessed over perspective the way I did.

Hindsight is 20/20, and if I could do things over again, I would have chosen another class. Finding classes and groups that suit me has made life easier. Rather than trying to change and fit into the mold of the accepting person, I accept the criticisms that help me grow as an artist while disregarding the rest. I've adopted this approach to critique for years and I've been a happier artist ever since.

Own your unique style and keep doing things your way. There have been artists in the world of all different styles and it's difficult to compare all of them. Allowing someone (however well meaning) to change your artistic style can send you on an alternate course where you're not being true to yourself or your craft. This is not to say that if you would like to paint landscapes in a different way you shouldn't accept advice. After all, the artist has in mind what they would like to see and may need help getting there.

The second type of fear is a fear of success. This may seem a little weird, but sometimes a feeling of worry will creep in about things going right! I've been concerned over the exposure I might receive. Since I'm more introverted, I wondered if I might become overwhelmed.

I was concerned that if I sold a lot of art I wouldn't be able to keep up with the demand. I realized later on that customers bought my work because of the time it took to create it. For me, having enough paintings to fill a booth at an art show or at least having a few for sale on Etsy or Amazon is adequate.

Other worries include scaling my operations if needed. Was I ready to increase the scope of my work? I worried that since I would have a limited amount of handmade items, I might have to produce them at a faster rate. I was surprised to find that the items I sold were of such variety that it was possible to keep up with the demand by simply making a diverse set of products.

In short, it was up to me! After finding an answer to this concern I was able to breathe a sigh of relief. Because making art is still a part time endeavor for me, it's impossible to "run out" of art unless I stop making it entirely. My customers are looking for diverse things. For example, some customers want winter pictures of trees and others would rather buy fantasy art.

Another concern I had was that the quality of my work would go down from trying to keep up. As an artist, I learned that by going at the same pace I was actually increasing the value of my work. Some artists are more prolific than others. As an artist, you can set the quality of your work to what satisfies you.

I enjoy a new challenge, so this year I began producing linoleum block prints. This enables me to print my designs in the quantity that I find acceptable. I price my prints so they are more affordable to more buyers.

– disappointment

The handmade marketplace has grown not just in the numbers of buyers but in the numbers of sellers. By 2017, Etsy had grown to 1.93 million sellers. I signed up for Amazon Handmade when it began and my early presence in that marketplace has resulted in more sales. However, even though I joined Etsy late, my participation effects my sales. I feel that when I spend more time perfecting listings my store succeeds.

As a result of this observation, I feel you it's possible to join a handmade marketplace late and compete with many sellers and still have success. It all depends on the seller's willingness to add new listings, work on their presentation quality and perfect their process.

Don't allow disappointment in a lack of sales cause you to close your shop. If keeping it open isn't a hardship, keep working on creating inventory. Try changing graphical elements such as banners and logos. Improving my Etsy banner and streamlining my listings down to my bestselling products resulted in additional sales.

In addition, scan your store profile. Are there some things that could be improved such as your artist biography? Perhaps have a friend, acquaintance or potential customer view it and listen to their feedback. In the past, I've seen handmade sellers offer an URL to their store so that others in the group can provide a critique. This has resulted in helpful suggestions, compliments and access to fresh ideas.

The following is a hint for Amazon Handmade Sellers. If you have an Amazon Handmade storefront, try switching out the banner in your artisan profile. Try including a couple products within the cover graphic with links to those products. Every time I've done this, an item sells because of the higher visibility of these products when the buyer views my store.

Business Plan

Once you have a goal in mind, like any creative person you just want to get to work. This is when I recommend taking a deep breath and putting it all down on paper. Take some notes of your ideas. It doesn't necessarily have to be in order, it's just a way to get your thoughts down so you don't forget them.

I never created a business plan myself, but if you like to be prepared and organized, this could be the best route. If you would like to benefit from the experience of professionals, I recommend SCORE. To find a chapter near you, visit their website at score.org. You'll be able to tap into decades of experience.

From the SCORE website: "We connect entrepreneurs with mentors to help you build your business with free business advice." I met a couple SCORE mentors in the community, and they're a great resource for entrepreneurs.

This is a business plan of sorts for those wishing to form a creative business. In my opinion, a boiler plate business plan template lacks a few considerations. The art market is a business somewhat based in reciprocity, and each market appears to have its own conditions whereby an artist can succeed. Artists have to be adaptable to the markets they're selling in.

With streamlining in mind for creatives, I'm only covering a few points of the business plan. A business plan is defined as a formal statement of business goals. It includes statements on why the goals are attainable and how they'll be achieved.

A first question to answer in your business plan consists of solving a problem. This can be a though provoking question for the artist, because the obvious answer is to effect viewers simply by being in the presence of art. Successful makers of handmade goods are ingenious enough to make their art fill a practical need.

I sell paintings for the aesthetic value to buyers, but I also sell more practical items such as wood burned coasters, screen printed pillow cases and linoleum block prints. When art has more than one purpose, the most practical buyer will be attracted to it.

Paintings have a decorative use, and looking at your work will allow you to find more purposes for your work by assessing it with an eye for finding practical uses. This analysis of your work can be a beneficial part of your business plan.

Target Market

A second task is determining what niche your work will fill. Niche marketing is the technique of targeting a specific sector in the market. For instance, if you're interested in creating art that those decorating homes in remote areas would buy, you might make art that appeals to this market. This is just an example. Research could reveal much more about the demographic your work would appeal to.

This leads us to your potential customer. Identifying your customer in the previous step will help you figure out the answers to the following questions. Who are your future customers, and how can you market and sell your products to them?

I've often pictured my potential market as a friendly group of art patrons who like my work. My target audience is rather broad. Be as specific as you like when trying to determine a group's taste in art. For example, if you make beaded bracelets, your target market may be women of a specific age who will be the most likely to purchase your jewelry. If these individuals like a specific breed of dog depicted in the beads of your bracelets, they would be considered a niche market and may encompass fans of the dogs in general.

Analyzing the size of your target market is a good idea. If you make a t-shirt with a slogan that appeals to a group, is it easy to determine how many customers would buy your apparel. Artists often take up causes, this being one of the most admirable aspects of what we do. However, with sustainability as a consideration, you'll need enough sales to support your business, so if your niche market is very small, it may be a good idea to add additional works to expand your reach.

While on the topic of research, it's also helpful to learn more about your competitors. I almost think the word competitor may not apply in terms of art, but researching successful artists producing work that may be in the same category can be advantageous.

I sometimes peruse Etsy to see the most popular, featured products. I often jot down what makes these products so unique. Reading customer product reviews can also indicate features that are appealing that may lead you in the right direction in terms of what a specific group is looking for.

Figuring out the needs of your target market is a great way to conceptualize innovations. I also browse the pages of art magazines and more mainstream periodicals such as Martha Stewart Living. Searching Pinterest can also yield some inspiration regarding popular trends.

I've found in my creative business that my contribution to the market is unique enough that I'm not concerned with competition. In fact, creative businesses seem to work the best when working together. Admiring and patronizing each others' businesses is welcomed. Organizing events together and celebrating diversity is a great way to encourage each other.

Learning the marketing approaches of others can provide a great deal of useful information. Studying the types of social media marketing approaches can be beneficial. Finding posts with many likes can serve as an example of what works whether it is in the content shared to the groups of influencers sharing the posts.

I often consider what I like and don't like about the marketing campaigns of others. I also visit quite a few blogs and social media profiles. I often consider the advice of others marketing the same types of products. It's a great way to test my theories and craft a polished new approach. I take notes of what I've learned as a result of research and incorporate these approaches into my own marketing plan.

Inventory

If you're in the handmade business, making it yourself builds truth with customers looking for original art. The reason why art collectors buy art is because it's a great investment. A painting, for example, is something created by the artist and of which there is only one in the world.

As an artist, you will need to make more than one to type of item to maintain an inventory of work available. Making each product yourself takes time and energy, but original works whether in the form of a painting, drawing, handcrafted jewelry or other artistic work are worth the most and should be priced accordingly.

One inventory consideration is selling in more than one channel. Items which you only have one of should be available in just one marketplace at a time. Selling high priced items on two or three selling platforms may seem like a good idea for added exposure. However, this practice requires a great deal of organization because when the item sells in one channel, the other listings have to be removed to avoid overselling the same item.

Multiple identical or similar items may be listed in more than one marketplace. When listing hand pulled block prints of identical design and color, I always mention in the product description that each item may have slight variations as a result of being handmade.

For those just getting into selling their handmade items, it can take awhile to just sell one product. My higher priced paintings take longer to sell, but I've sold many paintings in the $100 range. As a result, I paint more at this price point.

Making More Than One

There may be a time when it's worth considering selling more than one type of item. There are three possible reasons for this decision to be made. Firstly, it's easier to create one online listing for ten items compared to creating online listings for ten different items. I know I can pack more quality into that initial listing compared with the additional nine I may have to place in one day. When a task becomes repetitive, I pay less attention.

For those with a full schedule, selling identical items is a time saver. For products at a lower price, it can simplify the process. Each listing requires a set of photographs, descriptions to type, categories and keywords – and those are just a few considerations. Now that you've spent all day on this endeavor, imagine that each product is just $10.

Secondly, inventory becomes less demanding when selling products in more than one quantity. Not only is time saved in making a listing, inventory tracking just became easier. It's less complicated to keep track of ten items that are alike rather than ten that are different. By keeping lower priced items in groups, I don't have numbers of unique products to track. I have to admit, I get a little concerned when I look for a product I've sold and may not recall immediately what box it's in!

Finally, a seller might want to make more than one product because of Fulfilled by Amazon (FBA) at Amazon Handmade. FBA is a program that allows the seller to mail inventory to Amazon so that they may participate in Amazon Prime shipping. In other words, sellers send packaged and labeled inventory to Amazon in a box.

Labels have to be printed with a laser printer so that they may be scanned into inventory at the warehouse. From the warehouse, Amazon handles shipping and returns for the seller. There are videos with tutorials about how to participate within the Amazon Seller account interface and in the Amazon seller community discussion boards (to name a couple resources).

When the handmade seller wants to participate in Fulfilled by Amazon (FBA), having more items that are alike streamlines the process. Because it's challenging to begin FBA if you're new to selling on Amazon, beginning with many like items to sell can makes things easier. It may also be good for sales. A listing with ten items available presents buyers with the option of buying more than one of something they like. During big sale events such as Black Friday or Prime Day, this makes promotions easier to manage with more targeted results.

I have my own approach to selling more than one. I began my handmade business creating numbers of items, each one of them unique. I would come up with a different pattern for each item that I made. It seems disorganized to me today, but I was able to pin down the patterns and products I liked to make the best and which ones customers preferred.

Being me, I feel that running a creative business should be more entertaining than working a job that requires office attire. This isn't to say I would avoid making something when it's a big seller. Part of the enjoyment of operating a creative company is being fortunate enough to succeed and continue the work.

The products I make in a lower price range are becoming more uniform. One-of-a-kind items and custom creations like paintings can be unique if at a higher price range. By using this approach, I can continue to make original works of art, yet offer larger quantities of similar items to customers as well. This allows to offer customers using Amazon Prime more opportunities to buy my handmade creations in addition to saving time.

By having more quantities of a successful item on hand, sellers maximize both time and availability for buyers. That being said, items offered in more than one quantity should be those that are most likely to sell. It's difficult to judge which items to choose. The following is a list of recommendations for selecting items to produce more than one of. The items you select should meet at least one of these qualifications.

1. Products that have received positive feedback online (ie. social media or a website).
2. Products that have received positive feedback from customers at arts and crafts events.
3. Products that have sold in the past.
4. Products you can make faster than others.
5. Products that have been requested by customers.

You may wonder how alike these items have to be (because you're not a machine or one person factory!). Since each item is handmade, it's impossible for there not to be subtle differences. I've seen handmade sellers handle this aspect a couple of ways. Some refer to subtle differences due to the handmade nature of each one within the product listing.

Others emphasize the fact that the buyer is getting an item that may have a small variation because of the difficulties of the handmade process. Next, they describe how this is what makes it unique. As a result, the variations become a selling point. They are still selling the customer something similar in pattern to others, but with unique, one-of-a-kind features.

I have also seen product listings where a group of items is on display in the image. I'm divided on this approach because I like that it shows the product line, but I prefer it to be clear to the customer that they are receiving a single item rather than a set of items. I save product line pictures for my social media campaigns.

Printing Services

Assume you have a painting or illustration that you've decided to keep but would still like to offer for sale to the public. One way to share your work and make it affordable to customers is by having it reproduced as a print. Scanning at a high resolution is recommended, at least 300 dpi. Because I didn't have the funds to take my work to a service center to get it scanned, I used my scanner at home to scan portions of my art and stitch the image scans together in Photoshop.

You needn't go to this trouble. There are printing shops that can scan your work at high resolution for a reasonable fee.

Once I had the high resolution image file, I was able to upload the image of my art to a photo service online such as Shutterfly and have it printed online. There are numerous websites that produce quality prints of your work. Art can be printed on different surfaces such as canvas or archival paper.

I used a high resolution file of a geisha painting I had created and had it printed on silk for just five dollars. There are numerous surfaces to have your art printed on so that you can sell it everywhere and have a limitless supply to offer.

If you aren't ready to spend funds on professional prints of your work, you may want to consider one of the many print on demand (POD) websites online. Creators can upload a high resolution file to websites such as CafePress.com and RedBubble.com and receive royalties for each print sold.

Recently, Amazon launched a Merch website at merch.amazon.com where creators can sign up and upload their designs to be sold on t-shirts and other garments. Designers are able to adjust their royalty for each shirt sold. There is currently a limit to how many designs an artist can sell at once. Amazon apparently has a tier system where a designer can level up if they sell a specified amount in a certain amount of time.

There are many websites that allow artists and graphic designers to sell their designs to be placed on merchandise, and the websites offering this feature increase every day. A note on copyright: the designs you upload should always be your own original design. Even a phrase on a shirt should be checked for trademark to make sure you are complying with the website's terms of service.

Selling In Person vs. Online

Initially, I planned on selling both online and in person at art events. Everyone's experience is different, and I was no exception. At first, I began with more of an online presence. My first sales were on Etsy and Amazon Handmade. These sales seemed driven by my more popular social media posts.

It seemed that whenever I planned attending an event to promote my work in a local marketplace, I would run out of inventory. I decided to concentrate exclusively on my online sales for the time being. As my speed and work quality improved, I was able to accumulate enough inventory to cover both bases.

For me, it was convenient to begin selling online first. Other artists find that the reverse is the best way to begin an art business. If you're new to starting a handmade business, go with an approach that feels comfortable to you. Each has its advantages and disadvantages.

Selling online can reduce the inventory you have to store in your home, for instance. Amazon Handmade has a program for sellers known as FBA or Fulfilled by Amazon. This allows the seller to mail their inventory to Amazon after labeling their products and shipping them to an Amazon warehouse facility. A disadvantage of this is that there is a bit of a learning curve in learning how to package your inventory. Fortunately, Amazon offers many resources such as video tutorials and an online community of sellers who are helpful to new sellers.

Selling your goods online is a good option if you would like to pace yourself. Making handmade items takes time, and you may want need time to perfect your manufacturing methods before committing to a busy schedule. Producing inventory can become exhausting if an item is selling particularly well. Some sellers advise makers to adjust their prices or place a limit on custom made products.

Selling my handmade items online only for the first couple years of my business gave me time to build my inventory and see which of my products sold the best. In addition, I spent my spare time researching the marketplace, research online sell platforms, build and online presence and learn what works and what doesn't.

By the time I was ready to sell locally, I had more opportunities to take on the challenge. I had built upon my inventory to cover both online and local sales. I had built an online presence with websites and social media profiles to refer customers to. I also had accumulated many photographs of my work to share.

In addition, I had spent time learning new production methods. I consider this time period the most entertaining part of building my company! During the summer, I taught myself how to screen print with the photo emulsion technique. I spent the winter perfecting my woodburning. By the time spring turned into summer, I had learned how to produce linoleum block prints.

Each time I was able to display my newest work on social media, I was improving my marketing approach. Preparing my handmade business and building on my skills turned out to be less of a chore than I expected. It was the most relaxing, productive time I had ever spent as an artist. It's my hope that in building your own handmade business, you experience as much growth as an artist as I have these past few years.

Presentation

Before placing your first handmade listing or planning your booth at your first art show, it's important to plan your presentation. You'll need quality pictures of your work, a description of your product and an artist profile that communicates to the buyer the quality of your craft.

The following product images demonstrate types of images in a theme that I find effective for online listings. They also work well for websites, marketing materials and blogs. The following is a list of product views I often use in blog posts, on social media and in product listings.

1. A picture of the product in handmade packaging.
2. View of entire product (if possible).
3. A photo featuring the item in use.

The above image is of a set of four woodburned coasters with twine and a gift tag with our company initials. I created the yellow gift tag using a Cricut and card stock. The use of torn paper, prints or shapes cut with scissors work well with calligraphy or handwriting! Bright yellow cardstock offsets the twine and wooden coasters well. A splash of color makes a natural product stand out.

In the second product picture, I've demonstrated the texture of my product. Even if the image doesn't display the set of woodburned coasters in their entirely, it's a wonderful supporting image for customers who want to view the texture of your product. This enhances their shopping experience!

In the third product photo, I'm demonstrated my item in its entirety. This photograph shows a more complete view and even provides an example for its usage. These coasters are also a mandela puzzle! A fourth supporting picture might show a mug or glass situated on each one. Providing suggestions for how your product can be used makes it more appealing to buy.

Putting Yourself in the Place of the Buyer

Even if there is an established niche for your art or creative product, this isn't a guarantee that it will sell right away. With the expansion of the Internet, competition has increased. There are numerous artists offering their work for sale on the Internet.

This means that it's more important than ever to stand out as a quality option. Spending more time on your item's appearance is a good approach. Today's buyers are looking for something unique. Positive reviews from those who have purchased your art and have something nice to say about it can go a long way. Customers are also looking for something helpful. Art with a function is in demand.

I often put myself in the place of the buyer. Is your product something you would like to buy? If so, why? What are those features that set your product apart from others?

After answering these questions, I include these details in a product description.

Considering the visual appeal of your work is vital. Most art has an appearance that the buyer enjoys. Your art need not have a function other than hanging on the wall. If it makes the viewer relaxed, completes a room's decor, provokes a certain emotional response, this is all that's required.

If your creative item is pottery, it's likely the art work serves as a vessel for storage. This is a great selling point to emphasize to buyers who are looking for such utility in a piece.

Your production methods are another selling point. If your products are environmentally friendly, non-toxic or otherwise unique in a specific way, this is also good to mention. The size of an item will also interest buyers. Adding the dimensions is an important selling point. Your buyers need to know in advance how your art work will fit into their space. Include the materials used in the construction of your art, as this also influences the buyer because they may be looking for items constructed of wood or stone, for example.

It's also useful to the buyer to suggest uses for your handmade item. Keywords such as art therapy, rustic, contemporary, steampunk, modern etc. will help the buyer who is looking for these features in a work find your listing in a crowded marketplace.

After creating something new, I like to show my work to family, friends and other artists and ask their thoughts about it. This is a great way to gauge the future success of the things you make. While your family and friends will more than likely keep things positive, they can also point out the things they like, providing valuable information you can use to target your audience. With those appealing features in mind, you can create a marketing plan that will emphasize the positives about your products so you can market more effectively.

If you've found some weaknesses in your products, this is the time to close those loopholes and try again. If there's something that needs improvement, refine your approach until you feel you've created something that best represents your vision. As you've probably guessed, not everything you create will be a home run, and this may require some reflection or perhaps scrapping the idea entirely.

Your Online Listing

Buyers have an abbreviated amount of time to look at a listing. There are a sea of products they can view and they only have a few seconds to glance at your listing. To peak their interest and assure a sale, your listing needs to be superior than others.

Prior to listing a product, I usually scan the marketplaces I sell in, such as Etsy and Amazon Handmade for items in the same category. I also spend a lot of time of Pinterest viewing what other artists are doing. When zeroing in on images and listings from the most successful shops and artisans, I notice a couple features. The listing is described in such a way that is both useful, thorough and entertaining. In addition, the image looks great and the utility of the item is demonstrated in at least one of the images.

When looking at the online shops, stores and booths of others, think about what they are doing right and what they may be doing wrong. Take some notes on what is effective or not as effective about the presentation. These observations will provide an opening for your own original ideas.

I like to go on a bit of a field trip. By visiting craft shows, stores where handmade items are featured, art shows and gift shops I get to get out of the house and enjoy the beautiful weather as I do a little market research. I often purchase, snap a photo or write a brief note about something I found that day. Even if it's a packaging idea or a just a feeling I can embrace, all the better for my business. After my outing, I often arrive home feeling refreshed, inspired and ready to work. I can't emphasize enough how much a little fresh air to improve both your outlook and inspiration.

My listing goals involve a few things. Making sure my products meet the threshold for a similar or better quality experience is the first. Second, the product image has to reflect this. Product images should spotlight the item in such a way that demonstrates usefulness and appeal. The buyer should want to purchase an item not just because they have a purpose in mind for it, but they love the way it looks. Third, I like to add person touches to my descriptions such as minor points about the inspiration behind it, a glimpse into the process of making it and how it can be used.

Listing Components

The product image, product title, product description and keywords work as tools the seller can use to convert their listing into sales. Each component serves as an opportunity for the seller to maximize their product's visibility and show potential buyers how their item is superior.

Product Image + Product Title + Product Description + Keywords

A refined approach to each one of these components will impact the ease in which your item is found in an online marketplace and help your product get sales. An overview of each is provided in the following chapters.

Product Images

Product images need to accomplish a few things. First of all, an image should center on a problem the buyer needs to solve. If it's a scarf for example, it should look appealing as an accent to an article of clothing in the customer's wardrobe. It should also offer a demonstration of how it looks worn. A scarf on a model or stylish mannequin display is appealing and shows how it appears when worn. If these two aspects are addressed in the product photo, the chances of a sale increases when compared to a listing of a scarf situated on a table using poor lighting.

A product image should always emphasize the product being sold, but accents and props can be included as long as they do not steal attention from the item. One suggestion may be a small handmade jewelry accessory placed in the image in an understated way. Examples would be a nostalgic item such as wooden spool in a listing for a sewing accessory or dried flowers in a listing for handmade soap.

When photographing a painting, I like to provide three images.

One of a closeup of a portion of the painting so the buyer can see the textured brushwork, another of the entire painting cropped at the edges and a third of the painting on a wall. With these three images I have shown closeup detail, the product the buyer will get in its entirety and the painting on display in a setting.

Pictures should have minimal shadows. Indirect sunlight is also effective for taking pictures because full sunlight could make the image too bright or give your product too many shadows. The product shouldn't appear fuzzy. When taking pictures inside, a daylight bulb is recommended or a well lit area of your home.

In my studio, I have hung a set of lamps from the rafters normally used for brooding chicks. I have switched out the heat bulbs for 100-Watt bulbs. Using this in conjunction with the daylight coming in through the windows allows me to take flattering images of my products on the table without a photo box.

Additional photos are recommended with closeups of the pattern and material. A specific background to match the product image may be helpful. If your item is a large item like a blanket, try folding it in a variety of ways. Try to capture the product at a different angle. Try turning it rather than taking a picture along a straight line. Turning the product and taking a photo from a different vantage point offers a unique perspective.

The use of a light stained or painted vintage furniture piece can add visual interest. A buyer may recognize or appreciate the furniture when used as a backdrop for the product you're selling. A display may help them envision what it will look like in their own home.

These elements should increase the appeal of the product while not taking anything away from it. The buyer should be attracted by all the items in the image and have a positive feeling about each element. When your product image makes the buyer feel sentimental, inspired or hopeful, they'll want to buy it to own.

Before experimenting with adding props in your photos, refer to product image guidelines in the markets you're selling in. Some marketplaces like Amazon Handmade prefer that the seller have an image exclusively of the product with nothing distracting. With that being said, I have successfully listed items with a neutral patterned background and I've included small elements like dried flowers and burlap without being notified by Amazon Handmade of any issues.

If you package your items in a special way, using tags, string or other flourish, you can include this with the product image. For example, when selling screenprinted kitchen towels, I would wrap them in a kraft paper label with a printed logo on it. This product image provided the buyer with information about how they would receive the item. It didn't include any packing materials, so the item still looked handmade. This is just another selling point that adds visual appeal.

I have heard of other sellers being notified when their photos have backgrounds that are too busy, so a muted, neutral background appears to be best. Adding some texture in the background like wood, fabric or stone will also add some interest. In your marketing campaigns, this need not apply. Whenever I post in social media for marketing purposes, I group my products and props together based on a theme. I may even take a picture of the whole setting to share. Providing a link to my product listing directs the user to buy the item.

The images of your items should be high enough in resolution to look visually appealing on a web page. They should be large enough to look good to those reviewing your work on a computer screen.

Having basic digital photography skills is helpful. Another option is to find a friend or family member with some expertise to help you. If you're not under any time constraints, considering a photography class might be another option.

When it comes to equipment, it goes without saying that a new digital camera can be expensive depending on the brand and features. When I began taking pictures of my art work, I initially used a digital camera I had purchased at Walmart for about $100. While not top of the line, it took good product images in daylight.

I've had success taking pictures with my Android mobile phone on sunny and even overcast days. For small products, I use a photo booth constructed of five sheets of watercolor art paper. I taped the joints on the outside with clear tape so the flaps could be folded down when not in use. I typically take the homemade photo booth outdoors to make use of sunlight, but I've had good results with a table lamp indoors.

In a year, I've considered purchasing a photo booth, but my homemade solution still seems effective.

For a more rustic look, burlap or wood textures can be used as a backdrop. These types of backgrounds are appealing for Pinterest and Instagram posts. When selling bracelets, I've had my daughter wear it in a photo. This is an effective approach for clothing and accessories.

When presenting a product in a listing, I prefer to have the background be fairly muted. It doesn't help your item stand out if the background is busy. In the past I've also used natural looking props such as flowers, sage and pine needles. These items offer a natural setting that doesn't detract from my product for sale.

When it comes to editing images, I've used Adobe Photoshop for cropping and improving my product photographs. Although I still use this program for image editing, I mostly reserve it for graphic design work. Since I have so many product listings on a given day, I prefer the convenience of mobile apps. I currently use Pixlr for cropping images, but I have also used the features within Instagram to edit images. There are many other image editing applications that are free such as Gimp, an open source software similar to Adobe Photoshop in function.

Product Title

A product title should call out the most original aspects of the item it describes. Product titles can sometimes impact the visibility of your listing, dependent on which marketplace your listing will appear in.

Because algorithms on websites such as Etsy and Amazon Handmade change from time to time, it's recommended that beyond this book, artists should network with others who sell in the marketplace they wish to sell in. In addition, websites like Etsy have information about how their search functions. Amazon Handmade also has video tutorials and tips on best practices. Its recommended that handmade sellers refer to this information as needed.

The algorithms in this case can be considered as a set of rules that determine how information is handled and processed when search terms are typed in. Your listing could rank higher or lower depending on keywords within your product title and factors such as seller performance.

As an aside, seller performance is mentioned as a factor because it should be emphasized as a vital part of what will help you succeed. As an example, according to information on their website, Etsy's algorithms are configured to take shop performance into account. In other words, sellers who have more sales and happier customers can appear higher in search results.

Good titles say more about the product than an unhelpful one would. Product titles could be considered the most practical portion of the listing, and they include elements such as theme, type and the color. Product titles also include keywords. When it comes to creating a product title I follow a specific method. Comprised mainly of nouns, my product titles leave out rhetorical flourishes and saves them for the description where I'll have more room to add them.

Here is an example of a helpful product title:

Woodburned Spoon with Mushroom Design

This product title accomplishes the following missions. First of all, it identifies the item as "woodburned" which translates into a type of craft medium that is unique. Those looking for woodburned items will find this listing in the right category should they enter the term "woodburned" into the search. Secondly, the terms "mushroom"and "design" tells the buyer that the listing is for a spoon with a mushroom design on it.

Here is an example of an unhelpful product title:

Wooden Woodburned Spoon Great Birthday Gift Free Shipping

This product title is less helpful to buyers because it mentions the terms "great birthday gift" and "free shipping". It doesn't tell the buyer about the product pattern which might make it a great addition to their mushroom themed kitchen. Nor are these sets of terms needed because "great birthday gift" would make a better event keyword and "free shipping" may already be present in the listing and could be disregarded. Adding extra words wastes characters, especially if the keywords have been covered earlier in the listing.

The first product title example is better because it offers more opportunities for the product to be found. The wording builds on the product description, keywords and other aspects possibly covered in the website's features, such as a free shipping filter.

Product Description

As stated previously, it's helpful to mention in your product description the handmade nature of your creations. The product description provides room for details, but providing an organized overview at the beginning of your description provides the buyer with some notable features they may be looking for.

This initial overview can include main selling points such as more information about the color, the size (if it isn't present anywhere else in the listing form), the materials used and other details.

Buyers are often looking for certain features in a product description, and they want the most direct route to this information. Having a bulleted list will provide buyers with a opportunity to scan your product information quickly. A buyer that has to skim large amounts of text may be dissatisfied and move on to another item.

In my listings I have included a brief list that mentions the color, shade, the name of the artist and the materials. This makes the description more concise to read. Providing descriptive words in this list captures the attention of the buyer. If they happen to find an appealing feature within this list, it helps them add up the reasons why they should buy the item.

For example, what if the buyer is looking for a hand knit wool scarf in specific colors and each one of these features is mentioned in the first three lines of your description? The answer is, within a few seconds, the buyer has determined a few reasons to purchase your product!

Should the buyer want to know more about my shop practices or creative process, they can scan further down and read them in the longer portion of the product description. However, even if the space is allowed, I prefer to keep things concise because my artist profile is also working on my behalf.

Keywords

If you have mentioned some of the keywords about your item in your product title, you have achieved part of the goal in creating a keyword rich listing. While adding more keywords to your product listing, they should contain words that are relevant to your product listing. For example, I used the word "woodburned" in my description of my product.

Now that I've done that, there are a couple ways to refer to this type of craft. The term "pyrography" means the same thing to those buying and working in this medium. In addition, "wood burning" is another way to spell "woodburning". In fact, as I'm looking at my word processor, "woodburning" has a wavy red line underneath it indicating that it's misspelled. As a result, I often add whichever term I didn't use in the title as a keyword.

Keywords shouldn't be broad or overly narrow. A broad keyword will get buried in the competition, while an overly narrow keyword will be less likely to be typed into a search. More keywords that may be of assistance for my product include mushroom, wooden spoon, kitchen utensil, kitchen spoon and cooking spoon.

There may be many more ways to say "spoon", but better keywords could be added when describing this mushroom design. The mushroom depicted on this particular spoon is also a morel, so I may be able to add "morel" to my title or as a keyword. In addition, if there's a daisy in the design, I could also mention this variety of flower as a keyword. If the daisy is prominent in the design, I could add "daisy" to the title instead.

Some handmade sellers also include the name of the event the item would be best for. A woodburned spoon with a mushroom and a daisy on it would be a great gift for Mother's Day, so I might add this keyword. In the case of the example product, I would choose "rustic" or "primitive" as a keyword in the style section.

It's worth noting that Amazon Handmade has sections for style and holiday keywords while Etsy offers sections that allow sellers to designate a holiday, room and occasion. Filling out these areas is helpful. The more keyword and tagging sections that are utilized, the more visible the listing is to buyers looking for specific things.

Your Artist Profile

Buyers want to feel connected to the work they are purchasing. They may want to know more about the artist who created it. This information becomes part of the story. It's something they can share when discussing their purchase with others.

When creating an artist page or marketing materials, an image of the artist and their work are both important elements. Artists should have a good photo of themselves for their websites and artist pages. Handmade selling platforms often offer an artisan page.

The biography portion should communicate what inspires you as an artist. It can also provide details such as any art education or training you've had, how you began in art and what types of mediums you work in. I try to keep my information concise and just a couple paragraphs long. My biography includes details about my work along with a couple sentences about what inspires me to create.

I've changed my profile information many times. Etsy and Amazon Handmade both offer an artist profile feature. Every year,

I've updated my picture for my artist page on Amazon Handmade and Etsy. I've noticed that whenever I update my cover image with new art works, sales usually follow.

Viewing the profiles of other artists has allowed me to refine my own approach. The profiles I've viewed feature a friendly image of the artists at work in their studio or crafting space. Dress doesn't seem to be a factor in shop photos since the artist is giving information about their creative process. It's casual dress, work aprons, and paint splotches here and there. I've also seen artisan profiles where the artist is concentrating on their work in a meaningful way.

When I'm taking a photo for an artist portrait, I avoid the use of photo filters. Airbrushed effects can be great for creating a soft look for background elements, but I'm trying to communicate that I'm a real person that makes things by hand.

I find video snippets of the artist at work interesting. Social media platforms like Instagram have a my story feature where users can take a video of themselves. Beyond cementing the fact that your products are truly handmade, videos are successful as a selling tool because customers enjoy a demonstration. Like us, they want to learn more. Sharing trade secrets isn't necessary, but providing a small glimpse into your creative process allows the buyer a preview of what you're selling.

Social Media

Social media is a great place to begin advertising and it can be easy to manage regardless of the number of accounts. When I'm promoting on social media and I feel like I need to cover all the bases, I look for ways to create a single post that can be shared numerous times. Some social media marketers like social media managers such as Hootesuite, which with the cost of a monthly subscription will update numerous social media platforms at once. There are many other options similar to Hootesuite, such as Buffer, Hubspot and Sprout Social.

There are cost effective and even free ways to post to more than one social media account at once. For example, prior to sharing an update, Instagram provides you with the option of connecting to Facebook, Twitter and Tumblr. After connecting these accounts each time you post, these accounts will automatically be updated as well.

I often share my blog posts through my WordPress website. After writing and publishing a post on my WordPress blog, it's shared to my Twitter and Facebook pages automatically thanks to social media settings I have set within the Jetpack plugin.

When I find the time, I increase my participation on as many social networks as possible, but when I'm on-the-go, Pinterest and Instagram are my main focus when promoting my work. I like the pictorial nature of these options, since I'm mainly sharing images of my work. In addition, I have a higher social reach on these websites.

This isn't to say that Facebook and Twitter don't offer good image and video features. It's great to experiment and choose a social media website that's a good fit for your small business. Some marketers like to be everywhere, but I prefer quality over quantity. However, if the message is consistent and not watered down, it's great to be in more places where potential customers can find you.

When promoting your art on social media, it's important to add a description of the work, such as title and media. Offering a link for the user to purchase your work is ideal because some customers make an immediate decision to buy and you wouldn't want to miss out! For those offering custom work, adding a link to your store or contact information can be helpful for the customer who wants to place an order.

Unfortunately there's a caveat to social sharing for businesses. Much has changed in recent years as platforms like Facebook have changed their algorithms. You'll pay more for extended reach. Initially, small businesses were given higher visibility until social media platforms began to emphasize a pay for advertising model. The reach of business pages decreased.

Social media companies need to make money to stay in business. One of the ways they encourage businesses to buy ad space appears to be with algorithms. In the early days, my posts were visible to many users and then in some cases it ended up being just a handful after the algorithms were changed. This is unfortunate for the business just starting out without the extra stores of cash to finance long ad runs.

Some claim that organic reach has been reduced on Facebook due to changing algorithms that reduce the number of ads users see. The social media platform claims that these changes will drive more authentic interactions with companies. Facebook has also targeted engagement bait, or ads with direct requests for tags, likes and comments. Spam used to be everywhere on Facebook, and it still exists. However, these ads are often detected as such.

These changes needn't defeat your social media strategy if you're sharing engaging content. Introducing videos in your social media updates result in increased user interaction. After years of trying to build likes and followers, I've found over the years that it's not enough to have talent.

The most successful creative entrepreneurs are also savvy marketers who are adept at finding people that can help their cause. One approach that is free but requires precision and people skills is the use of influencer marketing.

Influencer marketing is a type of marketing that zeroes in on driving your brand's message to key leaders who will (hopefully) share your work with customers. Focusing on the most influential people begins with identifying them. They often have thousands (or even millions) of followers or are deeply involved in a topic online. They may also have expertise that drives people to buy what they recommend for an issue.

Once identified, a marketing campaign is then targeted around these individuals in the hope they will share your creations for sale. These influencers fulfill a valuable role in your creative business because they're promoting your work. Once a work is shared and discussed in a positive way, sales of that product begin.

Before jumping aboard any of the paid advertising options, it's best to get all the advertising you can for free. If you're considering paying for a Facebook, Bing or Google Ads, look into their promotions for first time customers. Some will give you a free amount to get started. The free promotion often allows you a budget of $100 or more.

This is an excellent opportunity to test drive which paid option will be the most effective. For example, you may discover that paying for an ad on Facebook is a boon because you'll sell more products to cover your advertising expenses. On the other hand, it could also confirm that going free is more cost effective for the time being.

I decided that I couldn't afford to spend money on advertising or worry about algorithm changes, so my tactic was to network more. Methods I used to boost my website include joining groups and sharing the URL, meeting people at events or even something as simple as passing out a business card.

Other ways to gain visibility include the use of trending hashtags. Encouraging other users to retweet and share your posts can sometimes be very helpful in increasing engagement. Networking with other artists on social media is helpful for finding others working towards a similar goal.

Networking usually utilizes a system of reciprocity where you may like or share a post for another artist, host another author on your blog, mention their work on your website or something similar. Artists can network by getting to know creatives in their own community and participating in events of mutual benefit to all.

In the next chapters, I will break social media websites down a little further. I'll explain how I use each briefly. A wealth of information can also be found by visiting the help pages on these websites. Each one of the following social media options have a mobile application that functions great for marketing on-the-go.

Facebook

For those who don't have a website yet, a Facebook Page can offer a free solution. If you already have a Facebook account, you are already set up to create a company page and make yourself administrator. From there, you can build an online presence to promote your brand.

I have a Facebook page set up to connect with users and promote my work. It's a great way to connect with fellow artists with similar interests, and it's one of the best ways to network I've used thus far.

Recently, Facebook provided a free store option using Stripe as a payment processor. As of this writing, this is something that may be in the test phase. I think it's a great thing, however, since I won't have to pay fees as I would normally pay using other shopping cart plugins.

Twitter

If you've ever watched the news or heard about a celebrity meltdown on social media, you've surely heard of Twitter. Don't let this intimidate you. Like many social media platforms, when used carefully, Twitter is a great medium for business social interaction. By the way, a post is referred to as a Tweet. You're probably already aware of this with the many blunders made on Twitter by people on the Internet.

For me, Twitter was this unusual social media website that seemed to have a learning curve. I was intrigued by the constraints of a character limit. As of this writing, the character limit is up to 180 for some users. This can create some challenges, but if you're a hash tag, abbreviations or acronyms kind of person, it can be quite fun to cobble an advertising slogan together and post it as a tweet.

As a marketing person, I don't like to drown in ad copy and your customer may not either. That's what makes Twitter interesting. It allows everyone a concise message. In short it makes everyone drop a paragraph to one sentence. There are ways around this such as numbering your tweets so followers know when the series has ended, ie. 1 of 2. I've never opted to do this as I prefer to stick to the character limit and add a visual.

Here's an example of how I format a Tweet (of course you're welcome to put Tweets together in a way that works for you, the following is just an example of a format I use):

Read my latest book Building a Handmade Business. http://website.example #topic1 #topic2 @writeartdesign

Let's break this Tweet down:

Read my latest book Building a Handmade Business.

This tells the reader a couple things. First of all, I have a new book. Second of all it provides the title of the book making it easy for someone to find if they were to enter the query in a search engine.

http://website.example

(By the way, this isn't a real URL I'm using, I just added it to the Tweet as a demonstration). The URL you use here should be a link to a blog post on the topic, buy link or website. If an URL is long, Twitter will sometimes shorten it. Users can save on characters by visiting free URL shortening services such as bit.ly. Typing in the

URL and hitting the button on this website will provide you will a short URL that can be copied and pasted into a tweet.

#topic1 #topic2

These are hash tags. They serve as a conversation starter on Twitter. It's a good idea to visit Twitter and search for hash tags to determine which most is the most relevant for your Tweet. Once you find a category, you can use it accordingly. On Twitter you are able to type in the hashtag and find all recent posts by users adding to the conversation.

@writeartdesign

This is a reference to a Twitter user name (in this case, mine!) Whenever a Twitter handle is included in a tweet, the specified user will get a notice of the mention.

It's worth noting that hashtags are prevalent on the Web and can be used on other social media platforms. In addition, a hashtag can be typed into a search engine such as Google where everything posted under a hashtag is available for viewing.

Pinterest

Pinterest is a visual social media platform that allows users to share and save images they find on the web to something of a visual bulletin board. A user creates a "board" with a title and saves images (referred to as pins) to it by using the save or pin button. If you like knitting for example, you could create a board entitled something like "Love to Knit" (or whatever name you feel describes the board's focus) and then collect images that have the same focus.

Boards can me made public, marked private or you can specify which users are invited to view and add to them. Each image item you share to a bulletin board is considered "pinned," and pinning happens all the time on Pinterest. You'll be notified whenever someone decides to share your contribution to their own own boards. This is how your product's visibility increases.

Like Facebook and other social media websites, Pinterest offers paid advertising options.

Clicking on an image on a Pinterest user board allows the user to visit the source of the image. If someone clicks on an image, they'll be taken to your website. It's helpful to type a paragraph about the work and add any relevant hashtags or information.

If I've sold a painting, I like to keep it on my board and then mark it "SOLD." This raises my credibility as an artist who has sold paintings. In addition to "SOLD," I like to add, "Thanks to the buyer!".

After using Pinterest and pinning images to your board, you may discover that other users will re-pin your image. This happens all the time on Pinterest and is the focus of the website. If I share art, I try to add a watermark with my name, year of creation and copyright symbol to identify a work as my own original idea.

Some ideas for harnessing the social power of Pinterest for your creative business include:

Create a Pinterest board for your art and share the link on your blog, website and social media. DIY is popular on Pinterest, with creatives turning to this medium to get ideas, tutorials and to share their work. The medium works well for artists as much of what we do is visual in nature.

Consider giving back by making an infographic about your business or industry. An infographic is a graphic similar to a flow chart that offers information. Helpful resources could possibly result in increased visits to your website or improve visibility for your products.

Instagram

I've been using Instagram for a couple years. It's integrated with Facebook in that you can follow your friends easily. In addition, you're able to post on Facebook, Twitter, Tumblr and Instagram instantaneously. It allows you to add text and hashtags but is more image based in nature.

When creating posts on Instagram, clicking the plus sign begins a new post. After selecting images, I like to use the Photo Booth feature (click the square which is divided into three spaces to install). Photo Booth provides access to different montage style such as images stacked in rows of three or four.

Clicking the symbol with the two squares stacked on top of each other allows you to post more than one image in order. For instance, my daughter likes to post her comic strip series one panel at a time. This allows the viewer to side swipe each cartoon image in the comic strip to see them in order.

Boomerang is a new feature that allows users to make and share mini videos using the Instagram app. When opening Boomerang in Instagram (click the infinity symbol), you're prompted to first install the application. Once it's installed, open it again allow the application access to shoot a video. Once a small segment of video is captured, Boomerang both reverses and speeds up the playback for an entertaining, quirky result that can be shared on Instagram.

What is great about Instagram in addition to these features is the photo filters offered. If you're not satisfied with the lighting or color balance in your photo, you can select a photo filter with names such as "Clarendon", "Gingham" and more. The Photo Booth feature will also find images on your mobile phone of a certain category such as faces.

Local Sales

Art fairs and arts and crafts shows are pleasant gatherings that provide an opportunity to surround yourself with what inspires you. Attending a local event is an opportunity to meet and greet potential customers in your area. Online selling is a convenient option, but networking with people nearby can increase sales. In addition, attending an arts event in your hometown provides you with the opportunity to meet other artists and crafters.

If you're an artist, it's important to subscribe to resources with community events you can participate in. Research is needed to discover a venue that's a good fit for your handmade products. Local newspapers, community bulletin boards at local businesses, Facebook social pages and your friendly search engine can be invaluable resources of information.

To stay informed, I follow business pages on social media that regularly feature arts and craft shows. Consider liking and following social media pages of artists in the area. They often share information you otherwise may not find anywhere else.

A local marketing approach I've been successful at is to offer my work for consignment at the shops in the area. Businesses often advertise when they're interested in adding handmade inventory, but I found an important venue by just chatting with a manager of a local business. This is another example where networking locally resulted in fresh opportunities. Clearly, the more places you can find to provide exposure for your handmade items, the more sales you'll have.

Even though I don't consider myself naturally outgoing, I've had success finding sales leads when simply telling people about my handmade business. One thing I am good at is talking to people in retail. These conversations often lead to me offering a business card or writing down my website. This is a simple tactic, because people are naturally curious about the careers and pastimes of others.

I speak confidently about my work because I believe in and enjoy what I do.

One of my more primitive methods for local advertising is a bumper sticker with my website URL on my classic, 1991 red and white Ford F-150 truck. Another similar idea I applied was using my Cricut to cut out a decal with the URL of my handmade website. The only catch to these marketing ideas is that I can't change these domain names because the stickers seem permanently planted on the vehicles. I'm certain a scraper will be required to remove them, but I'm not touching them. At this point, I find them a metaphor for sticking to it!

When it comes to outdoor art shows, many organizations operating arts and crafts events want to see pictures of your outdoor booth during the application phase. This can be hard to put together since you may not have had your first art show yet! My approach to this dilemma is to set up a canopy in the yard, arrange my handmade items on the table and take some pictures for as long as the weather allows.

Needless to say, this will provide you with some practice and a bit of a rehearsal. You'll be able to observe what about your current setup works and what doesn't. Outdoor events require special preparation.

I prefer a canopy with all four sides. This allows me to close the booth as needed. If you're not certain what the best type of canopy is for both the event and the needs of your business, it's good to do some research before spending hundreds of dollars. Read reviews on the different canopies available. You may find yourself willing to spend more on something sturdy. There are many suggestions for keeping your canopy in place on a windy day such as using weights to keep the poles on the ground.

Michelle Rufener sells at outdoor markets frequently in all types of weather and has good advice for keeping a canopy in place on a windy day. She recommends filling PVC pipe with cement and after setting the canopy up, attach heavy PVC pipes to the canopy legs with small bungee cords for a DIY stay-in-place solution.

Michelle also utilizes ratchet straps to assist in keeping her canopy grounded. During a storm, canopies can still be uprooted by the wind, but having a vented canopy for added air circulation helps. A white canopy is often recommended for art fairs, but even if white isn't your favorite color, it's still a good choice when it comes to a hot day. Dark colored canopies attract the heat.

There are many shortcuts that cut costs if you're someone who enjoys do-it-yourself projects. With that being said, there are many do-it-yourself options that can save money. Typing in "art show display ideas" into Pinterest will provide endless images and examples of fixes and display ideas. These ideas range from PVC pipe assemblies and collapsible wooden displays you can make yourself.

Running a booth outdoors can be hard work. Keeping your display concise, portable and quick to assemble will ensure you have enough energy for the event. Suggestions can be found by researching ideas that others have incorporated. Attending an outdoor art fair and observing how sellers handle various challenges is beneficial. Adopting the best practices of seasoned sellers will get you off to a good start.

Regardless of which approach you adopt to display your work, there are basic considerations that should be addressed whether the arts and crafts event you're attending is indoors or outdoors. The following isn't an exhaustive list, and it's likely you'll need to add to it or customize it based on your own needs.

Art Show Considerations

1. Your display should be organized.

2. Prices should be clearly marked.

3. Bring signs as needed (I find chalk boards or dry erase boards make excellent signs because I can change the messaging as needed).

4. Keep your extra inventory in a box until needed to replenish the table.

5. Keep business cards on the table.

6. Bring tablecloths for each table.

7. Keep a money box with change for a twenty (including coins).

8. If you accept Square or PayPal as a payment processor, your phone, tablet or PC should be tested and connected to the Internet.

9. Bring your sales tax license if needed.

10. Bring along a comfortable chair.

11. Bring along a lunch and something to drink.

12. Bring bags to place your customers' purchases in.

Your Website

Having a website is a valuable tool for placing your business on the Internet map. For those with home based businesses, a website can provide an address for your creative endeavors. Online marketplaces are a convenient place to sell, but having a company website, even if it's just informational is important.

Hosting is a monthly expense to consider. There are still some free hosts online, but most all of them place advertisements on your page. These unwanted ads dilute your message. Many webmasters monetize their blog, but it should always be up to you what ads are placed on your website. If anyone is going to profit from your content, it should be you.

Hosting packages can be very reasonable if purchased by the year. When I hosted through Godaddy, I found it to be very reliable for the most part. The hosting package I used allowed me to set up multiple WordPress blogs with a few clicks. This is a fast way to set up a hosted website.

Currently I used Blogger because although it's a free solution through Google, I liked the simplicity along with the integration with

Google products. I've had a free website at Blogspot.com for years. I even neglected my free page while I went through various hosting services. I find their Stats feature on the dashboard informative and easy to use. My pages get many visitors monthly, so traffic doesn't seem to be an issue.

Creating a Facebook business page affords businesses the same kinds of features a website does such as a shopping cart. It's a great early solution for sellers. The newly enhanced "About" feature allows you add more content. Facebook business pages allow for easy tracking of customer engagement.

When it comes to ecommerce solutions, familiar payment processors such as PayPal and Square are easy to use. They provide encrypted secure transactions for a per sale processing fee.

Square is a payment processing solution that I currently use. Buyers can use their credit or debit card to purchase from you using the complimentary card swiper they provide. This small square device hooks into the headphone jack on your smartphone or tablet device. You can also opt to buy a chip reader from Square.

Square charges a finance fee of about 2.75% per transaction. The customer can sign and receive a receipt by email. Thus far, my money has reached my account the next business day after a sale.

PayPal is a familiar brand, first gaining prominence on Ebay and then with buyers and sellers doing business online. PayPal is virtually everywhere, even in stores as a form of payment. It's important to take advantage of this and have an account ready to accept payments. PayPal also offers a mobile card reader.

Some handmade sellers prefer all-in-one solutions such as Shopify because it has robust features like inventory tracking, a payment gateway, unlimited bandwidth, advanced reporting and unlimited product listings.

These services each cost money whether it is billed monthly like Shopify or per transaction like PayPal and Square. Always view fees and membership costs before signing up. It's also helpful give the service a test drive before committing. You'll find that not everything will be a good option for your company.

Entering each item in your store can be time consuming, but well worth it. After listing over a hundred items for sale, I was weary from the constant repetition. It helps when you have more than one item because you only have to list it once and then just add the quantity. But how do you tackle listing fifty pairs of handmade earrings with slight variations?

If you're not willing to create more than one of the same design, copying and pasting from a text document may be helpful. I chose to write my listing title and product descriptions in word processor. Then I was then able to copy and paste the same listing information several times if needed.

Etsy and Amazon offer built in inventory tools that can help you keep track of your products. Each has reporting features that can eliminate some bookkeeping requirements. I once used databases for keeping track of inventory, but I found this too time consuming. Besides I wanted to get back to making things. I like the Amazon system so much, that I've adopted their system for creating product numbers for my items.

Since time is valuable, I'll utilize any reliable free solution that will save me time.

Selecting a domain can be fun but there are also some considerations. For example, I've used my name for a .com and this has worked rather well. My name is also fairly short, which is helpful. Consider using an acronym or initials if your own name isn't available. Keeping your domain name concise is important. Nobody wants to type in a lengthy domain name they can barely remember, so short and sweet is best.

It's a good idea to avoid some of the domain extensions. Some cost little to start but the renewal fee is considerably higher. A .co domain name extension can be three times the price of a .com when it comes to renewing it for another year. My advice is to research the extension you're going to use to find the renewal fees before you buy it.

Once you decide on your domain name, the next step is to forward it to a page. One fast fix while you're building your website is to forward visitors to your Facebook business page or online blog. It's also helpful in terms of saving money if you purchase a host that provides a domain for free.

Otherwise, keeping your eyes open for a less expensive registrar when possible. It's worth noting that at the time of this writing, Google Domains offers free privacy settings compared to Godaddy, who adds this fee on. If you don't opt for privacy, you may experience increased web spam such as unsolicited emails from individuals wanting to sell website services.

Marketing Materials

Business cards are still the go-to item for those times when you are looking to network with others in the same industry or pass out to potential customers. I've been designing business cards for years, and I still like the personal touch they add to my company. In the digital age, it seems like this mode of advertising may be going extinct, but I can assure you, this isn't the case. People still want something tangible, and business cards fulfill this need. My daughters used business cards as a backing board for some fimo earrings they had made to give away at our booth. We've also shared them in our booth, tacked them on boards featuring small businesses and slipped them into boxes with a customer order.

You may ask what's needed on a business card, but it's pretty simple. It's up to you! If you are looking to embrace a handmade marketing concept, one idea is to carve a linoleum block with your details and put your Cricut or illustration skills to work.

I always include the name of my company and the website URL at least. You can choose to ad an email address or a slogan. You can have your business card feature a QR code that goes to your website.

My most recent business card orders were with Vistaprint. Based on the quality of the cards I ordered, I felt that I received a good value for the cost and I would definitely order them again. It's helpful if you have a logo, but it isn't necessary if you decide on a template. The platform is easy to use and a digital proof is possible. Hiring a graphic designer to create your custom business card design is a good idea for professional results.

I'm sure there are many other printing companies, but another one I would like to mention is Moo.com. You can order half cards and square cards. The orders I've received are very high quality and you can design each card individually! That's right, each card can be different! Most online printing companies offer promotions that are ongoing, so be sure to look around for a code so that you can take advantage of the best price.

Shipping

If you're selling your art online or accepting orders from people you meet, it's likely you'll be shipping your work. When selling online, the platform you're using can impact your workflow, cost and efficiency. To calculate how much shipping is going to cost, you're going to need some information about your product such as length, width, height and weight.

The information is important because if you miscalculate your shipping costs, you'll end up with sticker shock and a total fee that will take a bite out of your profit. If this is a concern, it's important to do some research. Even if you elect to offer free shipping as a customer perk, calculating how much it will cost to ship packages is helpful in determining pricing.

Initially, I chose to take all my packages to the post office. This wasn't efficient for a number of reasons. First of all, I live in Michigan and traveling in a blizzard is not something you want to do. Online customers place orders every day, which means you have to be ready to ship them their order no matter how much snow falls or how icy the roads are.

Second of all, the post offices in my area have hours that change often. I've arrived at the post office many times to find it closed or on a lunch break. Even the information online about post office hours isn't necessarily accurate.

Thirdly, I ended up wasting time and money. There was one week where I brought the post office a bunch of business and ended up feeling very exasperated. I had used the wrong boxes, spent more than I should have, had to buy tape, etc.

I can't stress enough how important it is to keep packing tape on hand. Stock up when you can find it reasonable. You won't regret it. The situation that taught me this lesson was the day I walked into the post office needing a bit of tape to finish securing my package only to be told, "I can sell you some." And so she did at $2.99.

She used my newly purchased tape it to give my package a professional appearance, so I was thankful for that because taping is not my strong point. I used to be a stocker in a grocery store as a teenager, so unwrapping and un-boxing is more my thing. Needless to say, I learned that the U.S. Postal Service is not into helping you with your tape expenses, but they will sell you some. It's quality tape by the way!

Speaking of boxes, if mailing priority, make sure you don't "reconfigure" boxes from the post office. Recently, I had a painting to mail that didn't quite fit the Priority Mail box. I decided to give it a little more space by folding the flap an inch on one end. I was informed by the postal employee that on flat rate boxes, re-configuring a box isn't allowed.

My advice is, if you reconfigure a box, make sure it's a plain one!

I recycle boxes if I have an irregular sized item. I have mastered the technique of turning a box inside out when I need to. First, I remove any labels as desired and then separate the corner of the box at the seam so I can reverse it. I put the print side on the inside and tape it back together. This gives me a clean outside appearance.

Purchasing boxes is helpful if you ship an item over and over of a specific size. I sell polymer clay figurines that are roughly 4 inches by 4 inches. I bought several new boxes at Walmart for .48 each. They serve as a ready solution I can use immediately. My goal to ship purchases as soon as possible.

Rather than continuing to just use the Post Office, I've recently switched to printing shipping labels using both Etsy and Amazon Handmade. There are many positives about this. Both Amazon and Etsy seem to offer a discount for ordering your USPS shipping labels through them. Each also offers access to other shipping providers such as UPS and FedEx.

Etsy adds the cost of the shipping label to your Etsy bill while Amazon subtracts the fee for your USPS shipping label from the proceeds of your sale. For example, if my label to ship the item Priority costs $3 and the item proceeds are $25 (after selling fees are subtracted) than I would receive a direct deposit of $22.

I switched to an inexpensive laser printer that I found on Amazon for around $49. It's a monochrome printer that only prints in black, but it meets the needs of printing labels very well. The ink doesn't smear. Printing labels through Amazon and Etsy keeps me from having to spend money out of pocket every time I have a sale. By using this method, I'm able to pay the postage fees later from the proceeds.

While on the topic of shipping, if you're shipping your art work, it's important to do some research on best practices. Preparing to package your artwork is a shipping task you'll have to get used to as part of the routine of selling online.

I often recycle packing supplies from my online purchases to protect the art while in transit to the new owners. Canvases can be fragile, and I found a number of information resources that were helpful. Saatchi Art has a good article on shipping canvases properly at www.saatchiart.com/packaging. Incidentally, you can also sell your art work there!

My current method of shipping a painting includes making corner supports for the canvas from cardboard, bagging the art in a plastic bag and adding packing pillows or Styrofoam as needed. Be sure to include the packing slip and a thank you note for a more personal touch. I usually elect to send one of my many linoleum block printed cards with a "thank you" written on the inside.

Supplies

Any kind of business will produce supply expenses. In my early twenties, I was working in my parents' sports cards and collectibles hobby shop west of town. There was a lack of focus from the beginning.

Originally, I was going to sell my hand painted sweatshirts and t-shirts and my father was going to sell sports cards. Needless to say, the two themes didn't match so we ended up focusing more on one side of the business. In the 1990's, sports cards were ballooning in cost. By 1995, the bubble had burst.

We got caught up in growing our company in the wrong direction. This can happen easily in a small business. We kept buying things we didn't need. We purchased a new cash register none of us understood how to use. I sometimes imagine what we could have purchased with the three hundred dollars we spent on the register.

We could have at least went to more baseball games. That would have been considered research. The malfunctioning register represents a lesson learned. It would have been wiser to invest that money into inventory because that is what we sorely needed.

When addressing the needs of your business, don't be too eager to buy the biggest and best of everything. If you're in the arts business you may find that a sketchbook and some art pens would be the best thing to invest in.

Streamlined is the way to go. If you need a new laptop, consider lower priced models on the market if the need isn't great. Tech devices have a way of advancing so fast that things become obsolete quickly. It doesn't hurt to take a breather before buying something big. Be certain a new machine will contribute to your goal of building your company or take away from your bottom line. It's possible that all that's needed is an app on your phone or tablet.

Of course, if we would have started our little sports collectibles hobby shop in today's world I would have opted to use my Smart Phone, a Square payment processor and voila! $300 in equipment saved. Look around at what you already have, you may find a use for something you already own.

Recently, I found myself longing once again for a desktop for my upstairs studio. I didn't want to buy one new, but I did have a few things: a laptop with a broken keyboard, a USB keyboard and mouse plus an old monitor. The monitor was the bright spot because I had purchased it just before they began making a flatter monitor.

After configuring the laptop to stay on with the lid closed and plugging in the peripherals, I had created my own work station for free. Utilizing items already on hand equals more money to spend on creating inventory, the main purpose of a handmade business.

Tools of the Trade

If you are an artist who works mainly in airbrush, you'll have different needs compared to other artists working in different media. As a painter and artist who also creates wood burned items, airbrush art and sculpture, I require some specific types of tools.

It's good for your company if you read reviews on different types of equipment. For example, I read a few books and watched some videos before selecting the right airbrush to use. The costs of items such as airbrushes, professional wood burning machines and even screen printing supplies add up in a hurry.

What you need and what you require are specific to you. For example, you may decide that you prefer to create all your art work with a ball point pen on copy paper. If you like the outcome, than you may find that your needs are Spartan compared to the supply needs of a stained glass artist.

When I was selecting a pyrography pen for wood burning, I looked at the many options before deciding on on a Razertip Dual Woodburing Pen. After the initial expense of $200, I spent more funds on various pens. After my purchases arrived, I noticed that I didn't need at least two of them.

When making more expensive purchases for your business, it's good to buy what you need initially and then add on later.

Selling Fees

No matter where you post your work for sale on the web, you'll run into a fee. Fees become a necessary expense when selling on online marketplaces so your work can be found by more customers. Deciding how to adjust your price to accommodate fees requires planning.

I've decided that selling on Amazon Handmade is worth the ten percent fee because I pay a similar amount when I sell my items locally. While Amazon is a huge marketplace and it's easy for your items to get lost amid a sea of products, the sheer number of visitors on a website like Amazon is immense. In short, this is where many online customers shop.

Some handmade sellers prefer Etsy to Amazon Handmade and vice-versa. I've learned a great deal from trying both websites, and I have been equally satisfied with them. The items I list on Etsy are unique to those I sell on Amazon. I list more on Amazon Handmade because there isn't an insertion fee or renewal fee. This is a tactic that works for me. I like how both solutions handle seller fees, since I would rather see them subtracted from the proceeds before I receive any funds.

It's worth noting that some handmade sellers like to list on Ebay, but I find the seller fees hard to keep track of and let alone budget for. The postal rates are also higher on Ebay, which keeps me selling on Amazon and Etsy. Your experience on these platforms may vary depending on the needs of your handmade business.

Online Advertising

Advertising can be a major expense. As someone with a background in marketing, I can almost guarantee you that once identifying yourself as a business you will get approached by marketers. Should you believe everything they say?

That depends. If you've been visiting the Internet for awhile, you may have realized that not every review is to be believed. In an incentive for positive testimonial world, you can no longer accept everything at face value.

When considering buying marketing services or online ads, a question worth asking is whether what's being sold is something you can accomplish yourself. If so, you may need to decide whether this service will save time.

Amazon advertising has an advantage for those selling there because the ads reach the consumer on the website they're shopping on. This closes the gap between the ad and purchase. That being said, I've read a few success stories, but I've also read reviews that indicate the sponsored advertising wasn't necessarily adding the sales that were expected. I've heard the same thing about paid Facebook advertising as well. Based on what I've read, sellers seem to be divided on the results.

As for my own experience, I invested some money in Etsy advertising, but my sales didn't change. Ads I placed on Facebook didn't make much of a difference either. Advertising is usually a good investment, but making an informed decision before buying is best, because it's effortless to spend in the triple digits for an ad.

Before placing an ad that involves an investment, it's a good idea to have everything ready regarding ad text, sale information, link to the buy page and an appealing image of the product. Utilizing as many free ad credits as possible is a good way to sample the reach of such ads before spending your own money.

If you decide to invest in advertising, start with a small budget of $50 and monitor your success. If at that point, nothing seems to happen, then it's possible nothing will. If on the other hand, your sales are boosted and you have earned more than the ad cost, it's worth investing in again.

Time Management

If you're with me so far, I'm guessing you're a self starter. You can work independently and the buck stops with you. This is awesome in itself, but there are times when you have to delegate.

The best thing about delegating is, you get to choose!

An example of a real world situation is those times of the week when I have a deadline pressing down on me and my time is at a premium. Needless to say, the simplest jobs like cleaning fall by the wayside. I could hire a cleaning service, but most of us would politely ask our spouse or children to pick up the slack so we can get something done.

I'm fortunate to be able to rely on my family when I'm working hard on business things. To be sure, getting someone to do the dishes in your stead is a challenge, but can they help me with company stuff? As it turns out, they can! In fact, they may surprise you with their skills.

I've had family members work on illustrations, marketing and even bookkeeping. You may be wondering how in the world I managed to convince my teens that it was in their best interest to learn a business skill rather than spend the day gaming.

First of all, I like to think that I have some unique family members. I was able to motivate them to help by offering incentives such as credit for their portion and a share in the profits.

If you have some tasks you would like some additional assistance with and don't have anyone you know in mind to help, service marketplaces like Fiverr and applications like Task Rabbit can be helpful. A note of caution: be careful what you share in regard to trade secrets.

A Sustainable Creative Business

Keeping expenses down is vital if you plan on building a sustainable business. In the initial phase of a business with a small budget, it's important to keep a tight rein on expenses. In time, your creative business will evolve from initial brainstorming sessions into something more focused. As it turns out, the clock is ticking on your success rate.

Here is an undesirable statistic to consider. The SBA states that only 30% of new businesses fail during the first two years of being open, 50% during the first five years and 66% during the first 10.

For a creative business, this seems to indicate that staying inspired can keep your business alive beyond the first decade.

Pricing

Another topic to consider while building a successful creative business is how you'll make a profit. You'll have to consider the cost of supplies and the value of your time. If you're producing bracelets and the beads cost $10 and all other materials are an additional $2, plus it takes two hours to make each one; you certainly wouldn't want to charge $12 for the bracelet.

Depending on the quality of the craftsmanship, your creation may sell for a hundred dollars. Many artisans starting out will price their product modestly, and this may be a good approach if your work is relatively unknown.

From one artist to another, I think it's best to place value on your work. If this isn't a fire sale situation, don't put your work in the clearance bin. My daughter creates beautiful hand beaded jewelry that can be quite elaborate and she's received $100 for a bracelet. Considering the time invested, this is reasonable in my opinion. In essence, your work matters and it doesn't compare to the art of anyone else, so price it accordingly.

Pricing your products has a direct impact on the success of your company. If the price is too low, you risk losing money on it. If the price is too high, you may not sell it at all. Despite how important it is to price things correctly, it's also one of the hardest things you'll try to do. Placing a price on something I'd made by hand can raise all kinds of doubt about what your art is worth.

I've tried an approach in the past of selling my handmade items cheaply to see if I could build on my customer base quickly. Although I made sales, I earned little. I noticed something else. Whenever my items were priced cheaply, I received the following question: What's wrong with it? Then I watched in amazement as the customer moved on, deciding that it wasn't something they wanted despite their initial interest. When I marked the item up and then made some minor improvements in its appearance, the item sold at full price!

Whether you're keeping track of the time you spend on a project with an application on your phone or writing it down on paper, this type of record keeping will give you an idea what your product is worth.

Below is a single approach to pricing handmade items that I use. There are many other formulas, and it's a good idea to research more than one and customize an approach that works for you. Pinterest has many flow charts on topics such as pricing handmade items. Entering "pricing handmade items" in the search form will produce quite a few pins for you to save, consider and apply if desired.

The cost of materials refers to the cost of everything you use to create the item. Materials aren't just the yarn, paint, ink, canvas, paper, etc. you've purchased but packaging related objects such as tape. Labor refers to the time spent creating the item.

The time you spend planning the creation of the item should also be included as labor. If you're anything like me, you've spent hours planning how something should be constructed, what colors you'll use and sketching a plan. Profit in the formula below refers to a figure determined by you. This cost is the amount you would be comfortable earning from the sale of your original art.

Cost of Materials + Labor + Profit = Wholesale Price
Wholesale Price X 2 = Retail Price

Although this is a helpful formula, I've found the most complex portion is what to charge per hour for labor. My current approach is to make this hourly amount what I would make if expecting a rate per hour as if I was at work at a regular job. I use this amount and adjust the profit as needed. For example, if I feel my prices aren't competitive or they're under priced compared to items of similar quality in the marketplace I may add or subtract slightly.

When trying to find like items in the marketplace similar to mine, I sometimes question my price. You may also discover that something another artist has made seems to be priced less expensively than what you are charging. While it's natural to compare your work with other artists, always keep in mind your process may be lengthier, more exacting and more handmade. Before you start marking down your work, consider the next scenario.

A Tale of Two Products

The first product listing page features a moose print pillow case. The image of the product indicates that it's very cute. In terms of quantity, there are over a hundred available. It seems this product isn't going to run out any time soon and you may be able to wait for a price drop. In regard to the cost, it's priced economically. It's likely what you see in the ad is what you'll get (for the most part) when it arrives in a box two days later. The process to make the pillow case isn't described, but it could be assumed that this type of pillow case was manufactured in a machine.

Now consider the second product page from an artist's website. The moose pattern pillow case in the listing is described as constructed of 100% heavy cotton and the artist has sewn it together using a vintage Singer sewing machine.

The pillow case in the image features a charming moose pattern with pine trees around it. When you read more of the description, it states that the art on the pillow case is printed by hand from a linoleum block. There are two colors in this design. Brown for the moose and green for the pine trees.

The description of the item states how the artist has sketched the original design from their own imagination, transferred their idea onto two blocks (one for each color) and carved both of them by hand. In addition to all these steps, they rolled the ink onto each block and carefully printed one color. Next, they paused to let the first color dry completely before adding the second color to the whole series of twelve.

It took the artist all day to make all twelve pillow cases.

It's mentioned in the description that each one has subtle differences as a result of the hand printed process the handmade seller used. The ink may be heavier in some areas, but the pillow case has a sturdy look and the personality of the design reminds you of a simpler time. In addition, you can't get over how proud you would be to gift it to your father as an accent for his cabin.

Which pillow case would you rather own in this scenario? Is your preference the first pillow case, one of many? Or would you prefer the second pillow case, of which there are less than a dozen in the world being made in one day? I know which pillow case I would rather buy to treasure for generations.

When things are made by hand they have subtle variations because their making is a challenge. If I create twelve prints in one day, none of them are exactly identical. These are the one-of-a-kind features your customers are going to love.

This scenario was meant to illustrate how people feel about handmade products compared to those that may not be so handmade. Even if you don't go to the lengths described in your handmade process, I hope you place a good price on the things you make and understand it's worth every penny you're asking for it.

Perfecting a Process

When it comes to perfecting your workflow, it's a good idea to take notes. Through the process of trial and error when making your product, there are bound to be lessons learned that should be written down. It's possible that certain products perform better than others or using a specific design approach produces better results than a previous method. Because the new, more efficient series of steps will save time and energy in the future, write them down. I tend to switch projects often and I enjoy experimenting with different types of media. This doesn't mean I want to search for clues and re-learn each process over and over.

After trying to learn how to screenprint with photo emulsion for over a year, I discovered that when exposing my screen to sunlight, I liked the results better than when I used artificial light. After failing to write down how long to expose the screen, I had to re-learn this calculation when I went to screenprint a new project a year later.

Imagine the scene. I had to open the front door while carrying a box containing an emulsion covered screen with design art and glass stacked on top. Not to mention the entire preparation was covered in dark fabric so it wasn't exposed to the sun until I was ready for it to be.

All the while, my pair of shih-tzus were at my heels ready to play. At least they were enjoying themselves as I nearly tripped and fell down in the name of art. My dogs couldn't understand why I had to rush out the door at high noon with such an unusual bundle of stuff. Neither did the neighbors. I was still in my pajamas after all.

About a minute later, I had to rush back in and rinse out the negative space. Oops, the negative space never did rinse out. The screen was overexposed. Needless to say, I'm still far from perfecting screenprinting with the sun.

Making errors are part of the process, but the thought of creating another screen brings to mind the errors I made last time. I still don't understand why I try to accomplish things the hard way, but from here on out, I'm writing my future self a note to shorten the learning curve. However, the pajamas are here to stay.

Reducing Risk

Whether an artist or an author, we're all familiar with the idiom: starving artist. It can baffle the mind that things can get complicated for someone just wanting to share their creative work with the world.

Risk can come in the form of someone trying to steal from you or gain access to your personal information for purpose of fraud. Keeping things simple and following some basic rules is a good idea to reduce ways for things to go wrong. Keeping your operation streamlined is a good idea to reduce your exposure.

Recently, I received a message on my Facebook page that I had won something and they needed information such as my address. Although I do sometimes enter contests, this one didn't ring a bell. When I asked the messenger for clarification, they told me that mine was the winning bid at a specific auction website.

Once again, I responded with more questions. The individual responded with poor grammar and impatience when I didn't send along my personal details. Needless to say, they never got my address and found themselves marked as spam. The attack method was interesting. First, there was a sense of urgency. I had won something! Who wouldn't immediately pass out an address to get a prize?

A few years ago, I was also approached last year to donate a work of art I had spent considerable time on to a well known charity. At first, I was thrilled by the prospect of doing something good and the exposure my work would gain with the donation. After doing my research, I learned that the person soliciting my donation wasn't affiliated with the organization. This didn't sit well with me at all. I would rather donate directly.

Some situations are confusing. I was alerted more than once of websites that were selling my handmade products for high prices. After checking my records, I discovered I had made some consecutive sales and they were paid in full and sent to one address. These items were now appearing on a retail website at a markup. Had my work simply been purchased as inventory? It seems likely. I've concluded that it's possible I need to raise my prices since my work was obviously priced low enough to be re-sold to a third party. It's worth noting that businesses can sell products at wholesale prices and I suspect this is what happened.

In another case, my work and other works by other artists were found on a retail website. This turned out to be an affiliate website for Amazon. If you post images of your work online or sell online, you are bound to run into these situations.

If you determine that your copyright has been violated or retail fraud is taking place, it's best to act. Filing a complaint, communicating with others impacted and sending a cease and desist letter are just a couple actions to take.

These are the types of challenges you'll run into. Some situations are annoying and some are refined fraud attempts. Some fraudsters are looking to steal account access. More often than not, my account hasn't been compromised, but a phishing attempt has taken place. For example, I sometimes receive an email from "PayPal" letting me know I've made a substantial purchase.

The scammers behind this email are hoping I'll panic and "login" using their phony phishing page. If I fall for this trick, they'll immediately steal my password so they can take over my account. A good way to tell these are fraud attempts is by the email address and the fake URL in the email. None of them are a part of paypal.com, but a variation. The bad grammar is another signal. Companies like PayPal.com aren't going to send you a message with errors. They have professionals working for them to make sure their messaging is precise.

As a public facing business, it's hard to find a positive in being offish in the global marketplace. On one hand, you want to be accessible. On the other hand, you don't want everyone to know your home address if say, your business is home based. You can be assured that fraudsters are trying to exploit your dilemma. This isn't to say I advocate staying hidden, but trusted companies I order from and the customers I sell to have what they need to contact me.

As more and more entrepreneurs move their operations online, it's good to be aware of emerging security threats. Companies are getting hacked more and more frequently, so the security of your transactions online should be a consideration. There are some low cost ways to secure your communications based on common sense.

For example, when I register a domain name, I prefer keeping my registration details private. At the time of this writing, Google offers privacy service for free with a domain purchase. Virtually all domain name registrars offer to keep your details private for a fee. Imagine if everyone who wanted your address simply looked at your domain registration information? It might make you uncomfortable to receive both snail mail and email spam from third parties.

Ever since I began buying domains, I've received email from those wanting to sell me web design and search engine optimization services. Hitting the junk mail button on these random messages slows them down until next time. For peace of mind, enable two step authentication on your email account to keep unwanted individuals out.

As the person in charge, you have the final decision on what services you select and what supplies you purchase. Small business owners should be certain they are dealing with a company with a good reputation. If the name is unfamiliar, research is needed before proceeding. It's important to read reviews and ask questions.

Look for proof of trust in that company before buying, whether through registration with an overseeing entity or membership with a group that maintains integrity. Positive feedback from a reputable consumer website is another type of assurance. In addition, it should be easy to contact this entity about your transaction. Checking the warranties offered on goods purchased for your business and reviewing cancellation policies for services and memberships can save on misunderstandings. Proceed with the offer only if the terms are agreeable to you.

While on social media, you'll see many ads. In my experience, even a free resource has a catch and sometimes results in a high pressure sales situation. Being conservative with private details until you feel comfortable with the pitch can lessen your worries.

On Facebook, I've seen quite a few "free" offers for creative entrepreneurs. Many of these operate on a model of signing up with email, downloading a free ebook and then signing up for a free webinar. After looking over the information, I've found some of it helpful but each has a common thread. They're selling something. There isn't much of a problem with this because the product or service may prove very helpful. Nevertheless, it should be understood that the goal of the resource is to support the sale of products and services.

The resources promote an art supply that is supposed to be a breakthrough, an art class you can't make it without or a marketing webinar that will reveal all the secrets of selling. I usually step back when the sales pitch begins and begin my research on the company if I'm interested in the product or service. Otherwise, I just ignore it and move on.

I once listened to a salesman pitch his financial services to a couple of senior citizens at a casino. The one thing that amazed me was how he didn't let them talk. He monopolized the conversation to the point that I'm uncertain he even understood the financial needs of his audience. They were stuck listening to him because somehow they thought this person knew more than they did. This may not have been the case, since much of the conversation revolved around his golf game.

An important question to ask is whether you need what's being sold. If the price is reasonable, recommended by your peers and will result in a positive experience, it could be rewarding.

Caution is required when it comes to purchasing marketing services. Promises of sales beyond your wildest dreams should be met with skepticism. Before spending money, consider how hard it is for you to market your handmade items yourself. If you lack the time or face difficulties when making an interesting blog post or creating an effective status update on Facebook, then perhaps you could benefit from some basic services.

Keeping a list of requirements is a good way to avoid adding an additional bill that isn't needed. For instance, I wouldn't need a painting class because I'm satisfied with my style. However, I would enjoy the positive experience and it wouldn't cost much. Whether I take the class or not for personal enrichment and networking with other artists is up to me.

The needs of a creative business vary, but assessing your resources and skills is a good idea and will help you determine what could be helpful compared to what would be frivolous. Each community of sellers and buyers is unique. Altering your approach when marketing to these changing communities
is important as marketplaces grow and mature.

When considering the products or services in a social media ad, reading user comments can offer a lot of information. Although these can't always be trusted, it's good to note whether the remarks are predominantly positive or negative in nature. Whether or not the company is professional is often demonstrated in the way they respond to negative remarks.

Often, a company representative has replied to the comment by requesting more information. The tone is usually polite even to the more negative remarks. This indicates the company takes responsibility for errors, is responsive to customers in the event of an issue and keeps their cool under pressure.

Staying Informed

Keeping up with industry news is important for any venture. Business owners must identify new trends so they can produce products that create sales. I have an news application that allows me to read on specific topics such as self-publishing, handmade trends and home based businesses. I like to stay up to date on what's driving handmade sales in a number of areas.

Subscribing to news about websites like Amazon and Etsy can provide important information about changes that could impact revenue. I like to be aware of increasing fees, additional visitor traffic or new features within my seller account. These changes can alter my bottom line, so I like to know about them in advance.

When it comes to selling art, I look to Facebook groups comprised of handmade sellers, newsletters from Etsy and Amazon Handmade, and the local newspaper.

Handling Growth

Growth is the best kind of problem to have! When I was starting out I had many good ideas, but not all of them were sustainable. Creating a plan for the time your business will succeed is a good way to prepare for supply and production issues as they arise. It can be very stressful when you become overwhelmed, and you wouldn't want to be the handmade seller who became overextended and ended up with disappointed customers.

With your business receives an increase in sales, it becomes necessary of keep materials needed in stock and find suppliers able to provide adequate amounts of the materials required to successfully complete your orders.

Custom Orders

Some handmade sellers choose to avoid selling custom made orders initially, and I was one of them. I waited two years before offering a customized product until a customer requested a custom painted saw blade. Creating this custom order was such a pleasant experience and I enjoyed painting the subjects so much that I've added this option to my shop.

If you decide to sell a custom item, first practice making it a few times. Make a note of the supply brand, place you purchased it from and how much it cost. Set a timer to determine how long it takes to make each one. After making a few, you'll most likely know how many you can make available to your customers at one time.

If it's necessary to order supplies when an order is placed, choosing the fastest route such as Amazon Prime or a similar two day shipping service can be vital. Calling stores nearby or checking their websites for availability of a product is also a good idea. There are times when a one hour drive saves time and money on shipping, especially when working under a deadline.

When listing items that are made by custom order, I consider the time it takes to create the item compared to how much time I have available. For instance, if I have an obligation, I subtract this time from my available production time. These factors change the amount of custom orders I can accept.

I only offer a certain quantity of items for custom order at once. If I can make ten items within a week, I adjust the quantity to ten and set the lead time to fourteen days. I use this calculation because I like to provide myself with an extra seven days to order materials should I make errors or something happens to the supply of materials I have on hand. Thus far, I've been able to ship things to customers early.

The extra seven days guarantees the customer will receive their order on time and in good shape. In addition, it also provides me with more time if more than one custom item is ordered at once. Naturally, depending on how long it takes to make your unique craft, your production time will vary. Handmade selling platforms allow you to select the number of days to create the product that works best for you.

Circumstances also dictate the quantity of custom orders I can sell. If I'm having a good week and I am producing products at a rate higher than expected, I can offer more. If I experience a personal emergency, I can decrease the quantity if these orders haven't already sold out.

Canceling Orders

The cancellation of orders is usually available but may affect how your shop is reviewed.

I've heard from handmade sellers who have been in this unfortunate situation. They have notified their customers of the cancellation as soon as possible and explained some of the details behind it. For the most part, the customers have been described as sympathetic.

This makes sense because of the authentic nature of handmade. Makers are real people who participate fully in their craft. More often than not, there is no one to do the exact type of work if we can't. In one situation I learned about, the buyer allowed the seller more time to make the custom item because they really wanted the piece.

Vacation Mode

Coffe break!

It's hard to give advice on what I would do in every situation because sometimes life events can alter everything. Handmade sellers using Etsy and Amazon Handmade who have experienced health issues or other emergencies can put their store in vacation mode. This means you are effectively closing your online shop and hanging up a closed sign for the time being. The online selling platform or ecommerce solution used should offer this feature.

Placing a store in vacation mode is another option when things go wrong. While this impacts the number of visits to your store in the future, it may be necessary to take a break. Handmade sellers with shops online have reported declining pages visits and lackluster sales when re-opening their shop after a vacation, but it's possible to rebuild once things are settled.

It's a difficult decision to postpone a source of income and potential opportunities when your handmade store is new. However, closing shop for awhile while you attend to important matters is better than risking an unhappy customer and a stressed out you. During these times, it's best to focus on your needs and make sure those closest to you are okay.

Your Finances

Even before you begin to earn money, it's important to keep track of expenses. Once you make a sale, you'll need to save that information as well. Using records in your bank account, PayPal, Amazon Seller account, Etsy account, etc. will provide an immediate set of records that will be helpful if you choose to do your own bookkeeping.

If software is preferred, there are many quality bookkeeping solutions. Some are from well known companies like Quickbooks. Numerous options are available. A preliminary search on Google reveals many standard choices along with solutions especially for handmade businesses. Easy to use solutions are ideal. Helpful bookkeeping solutions with features such as cloud-based back-up, a user friendly interface and the straight forward categorization of expenses are ideal.

As an example, Quickbooks Self-Employed offers excellent support with a mobile application that is easy to use. For those concerned about quarterly taxes, Quickbooks Self-Employed keeps a running total of your estimated quarterly tax payment.

It's also helpful if your financial records can be backed up to a cloud-based server in case of hardware failure or other occurrence. The best bookkeeping software should make taxes easy to file, provide inventory features and categorizes your expenses in a way that makes sense.

Some solutions offer integration with websites such as Etsy and PayPal. Many accounting solutions like Godaddy Online Bookkeeping (formerly Outright) are reasonably priced and integrate with PayPal and banks.

Bookkeeping applications vary and are useful according to user requirements. I have tested Godaddy Online Bookkeeping and found it helpful at first. After using it awhile, I found errors such as expenses being categorized as sales. I also used Quickbooks Self-Employed for the trial period. I found that it worked well but I didn't want to spend the money for the version I needed.

After giving up on these options, I created a spreadsheet for my accounting needs. I began utilizing the reports generated by Etsy, Amazon, Paypal and my banking apps and enter the totals into my spreadsheet as needed. This system of accounting is effective for my needs, but I'm always willing to revisit the topic should I find a better solution. Since my business is a sole proprietorship, my situation isn't as complicated as someone with another type of business.

To get off to a good start, it's important to save records or receipts for products and services you purchase for your business. If saving receipts seems like a hassle, there are apps that can assist in keeping track of these transactions in a digital format. Often, I'm able to scan a QR code or barcode in a store shopping application to make a digital record of it.

I would like to emphasize that despite the manner in which I've simplified my bookkeeping methods, your business will face different challenges based on the types of products you sell, if you hire employees and the overall organization of your business.

Because financial issues can be complex, you'll want to get advice from an accountant as needed. Asking advice from those in the business community may also simplify things. Your local SCORE Association (www.score.org) has volunteers that can provide invaluable expertise on many small business topics. I've also found great resources for small businesses on the internet such as the Small Business Administration (www.SBA.gov).

Your Creative Story

You may have guessed that while you were planning your handmade shop and the products you would create to fill it, you were writing your own creative story. You are building the story of a brand, your brand. Taken together, your products, your work space, your creative process and your inspiration tell a background story about the types of products you create and why you create them.

Consider what makes your creative story unique before making brand decisions like the title of your shop, your company name or what your logo should look like. You may decide to craft your own message or hire someone who can assist with the details depending on the challenges you face, but your thinking about your creative story will get the ball rolling.

If there's anything I've learned, it's good to take some time to consider your brand. If you begin with what makes your creative story unique based on your experiences messaging. It won't be long before you're ready to choose a name for your business.

Lingering Questions and Doubts

Q. How long will all this take?

Most of us are familiar with the phrase, "slow and steady wins the race" from the Aesop's Fable, "The Tortoise and the Hare." It's a story about a race between a fast moving rabbit and his slow moving counterpart, the tortoise. The tale illustrates the importance of consistency and perseverance over speed.

I apply this philosophy to the creation of my art and to the way it's presented. This doesn't have to be every artists approach. How your art is created is up to you, but I feel it's important to not rush through your approach to buyers.

In other words, when it comes to setting up your presentation and promoting your work, you should be ready to run a marathon rather than a sprint. My first art sale took longer than I expected, but when it happened, it was exciting!

Q. What can I do while I'm waiting for a sale?

Before starting a business, I wanted to show my work to the public. Throughout my life, I've felt my work has brought happiness to those that viewed it. I was even able to teach others about creating art, and that made me feel great. When considering the altruistic goal of creating art as a benefit to others, the sale of an art work that earns money becomes an amazing perk of the whole experience.

It's good to take some time away from worrying about selling and get back to creating for yourself. You may just discover your next bestseller for the Christmas season.

Another helpful activity is to work on your marketing approach. At first, I was trying to sell everywhere at once, and it was creating fragmented results. It was only when I took a deep breath and concentrated my efforts on one endeavor at a time did I begin to see real results. I spent some time putting more effort into my website. I stopped focusing on selling platforms that weren't working and fine tuned my Etsy and Amazon Handmade stores. My efforts resulted in the sales that I'd been missing.

Q. Why haven't I had as much success as others?

Initially, I was in a hurry to have the same success as others doing similar work. I was under the impression that undoubtedly, I should be able to immediately expect the same success. In my mind, this theory should have worked. I have since determined that YMMV (acronym for Your Mileage May Vary) is a better description of the journey.

The success an artist will experience may look nothing like what you've read or heard because there are variances in the types of work each artist creates. In other words, it may take longer for an artist to find their audience.

Q. What if I'm wasting my time and setting myself up for failure?

Failure is the number one fear of most entrepreneurs, but I think a more frightening prospect is regret. When I think about how far I've come and all the hardships I've faced, I can't imagine a scenario where I never tried.

Sharing your art takes guts. It's a brave first step, one that many never endeavor to take. By making the decision to sell your creative work, you've already won! With this in mind, picture the expression on the face of your first paying customers when they display your art in their home or receive it as a gift.

Despite any doubts you've had, you're not wasting your time. When your first sale arrives, even if it's a modest one, celebrate it. Someone has decided that your work is something special. Take a deep breath and congratulate yourself because this isn't where the journey ends. You're on your way!

**"You're off to Great Places!
Today is your day!
Your mountain is waiting,
So... get on your way!"**

- Dr. Seuss, *Oh, The Places You'll Go!*

Acknowledgments

I would like to thank my family for listening to my ideas all these years. A special thank you to my grandmother, Blanche Pearl Arnold for keeping me distracted with arts and crafts so I could embrace my inner nerd. I would also like to offer my thanks to my cousin, Michelle for giving me both inspiration and feedback. A sincere thank you to my brother, Billy and my daughters, Jessica and Lisa for keeping the house together when I'm creating. I would also like to thank my father, William Arnold, Sr. for carrying on the tradition of making things by hand.

About the Author

Patricia Arnold is a versatile author who enjoys writing and illustrating books. She has written over a dozen books in various genres including fantasy fiction. Her first book, *Strictly G.I.* Is a WWII memoir. She lives in Northwest Michigan and has degrees in graphic design and marketing. Patricia has a Master's Degree in Information Assurance from Davenport University.

Facebook: facebook.com/writeartdesign/
Twitter: @writeartdesign
Instagram: @writeartdesign